Parade of Stories

compiled by ESTHER M. BJOLAND

revised by ANNE NEIGOFF, *Managing Editor*

STANDARD EDUCATIONAL CORPORATION   *Chicago 2003*

Library of Congress Cataloging in Publication Data

Bjoland, Esther M   ed.
   Parade of stories.
   SUMMARY: A selection of stories, folk and fairy tales,
and poems by such authors as Elizabeth Coatsworth, H. C. Andersen,
R. L. Stevenson, Rachel Field, and others.
   First published in 1954 under title: The story parade.
   1. Children's literature (Collections)
1. Literature—Collections I. Neigoff, Anne.
II. Title.
PZ5.B488Par5   808.8'99282   73-3180
ISBN 0-87392-005-8

Design and art direction by Willis Proudfoot

AA - 3

ACKNOWLEDGMENTS

We wish to express our deep thanks and appreciation to the following publishers, authors, and agents whose permission to use and reprint stories, poems, and—in the case of the Shepard drawings—illustrations has made this book possible.

THE BOOKHOUSE FOR CHILDREN and OLIVE BEAUPRÉ MILLER—for "Circus Parade" by Olive Beaupré Miller.

CURTIS BROWN, LTD., LONDON—for foreign rights for the illustrations by Ernest H. Shepard for "Pooh Goes Visiting and Gets into a Tight Place"; and for foreign rights for the text of Osmond Molarsky's "Song of the Empty Bottles," reprinted by permission of Curtis Brown, Ltd., text copyright ©1968 by Osmond Molarsky.

JACK CONROY — for "The Boomer's Fast Sooner Hound." Adapted by the author from "The Boomer Fireman's Fast Sooner Hound," by Jack Conroy from A Treasury of American Folklore, edited by B. A. Botkin, New York; Crown Publishers, 1944. Used by permission of Jack Conroy.

MARY CAROLYN DAVIES—for her poem "The Day Before April."

DOUBLEDAY & COMPANY, INC. — for "The Velveteen Rabbit" from The Velveteen Rabbit by Margery Bianco, reprinted by permission of Doubleday, Inc.; and for "The Animal Store" from Taxis and Toadstools by Rachel Field, copyright 1926 by Doubleday & Company, Inc.; and for "The Child Next Door" from Fairies and Chimneys by Rose Fyleman, copyright 1920 by Doubleday & Company, Inc.; and for "Mrs. Brown" from The Fairy Green by Rose Fyleman, copyright 1923 by Doubleday & Company, Inc.; and for "Yonie Wondernose" from Yonie Wondernose by Marguerite de Angeli, copyright 1944 by Marguerite de Angeli, reprinted by permission of Doubleday & Company, Inc.

E. P. DUTTON & CO., INC. — for text and illustrations for "Pooh Goes Visiting and Gets into a Tight Place" from the book Winnie-the-Pooh by A. A. Milne, illustrated by Ernest H. Shepard, copyright 1926 by E. P. Dutton & Co., Inc., renewal 1954 by A. A. Milne, used by permission of the publishers; and for "Spring Rain" from the book Around and About by Marchette Chute, copyright 1946 by Marchette Chute, copyright 1957 by E. P. Dutton & Co., Inc., reprinted by permission of the publishers.

HARPER & BROTHERS — for "Autumn Woods" from A World To Know by James S. Tippett, copyright 1933 by Harper & Brothers; and for "Trains" and "Ferry Boats" from I-Go-A-Traveling by James S. Tippett, copyright 1929 by Harper & Brothers; and for "The Sugar Snow" from The Little House in the Big Woods by Laura Ingalls Wilder, copyright 1932 by Harper & Brothers.

WILLIAM HEINEMANN, LTD., LONDON — for foreign rights for "The Velveteen Rabbit" by Margery W. Bianco.

LOTHROP, LEE AND SHEPHERD CO.—for "Dorrie and the Weather-Box" by Patricia Coombs, reprinted by permission of Lothrop, Lee and Shepherd Co., copyright ©1966 by Patricia Coombs.

METHUEN & CO., LTD., LONDON—for foreign rights for the text of "Pooh Goes Visiting and Gets into a Tight Place" from Winnie-the-Pooh, courtesy A. A. Milne, Methuen & Co. Ltd., London.

G. P. PUTNAM'S SONS — for "The Old Woman and Her Pig" from English Fairy Tales by Joseph Jacobs, copyright 1910, used by permission of G. P. Putnam's Sons; and for "Whistles," reprinted by permission of G. P. Putnam's Sons from Here, There and Everywhere by Dorothy Aldis, copyright 1927, 1928, 1955, 1956 by Dorothy Aldis.

RAND MC NALLY & COMPANY — for "Sonny-Boy Sim" from Sonny-Boy Sim by Elizabeth W. Baker, copyright 1948 by the Container Corporation of America and published by Rand McNally & Co.

THE SOCIETY OF AUTHORS, LONDON—for foreign rights for "The Child Next Door" and "Mrs. Brown" by Rose Fyleman, reprinted by permission of The Society of Authors as the literary representative of the estate of the late Rose Fyleman.

STORY PARADE, INC.—for "One Cold Day" by Elizabeth Coatsworth, copyright 1952 by Story Parade, Inc., reprinted by permission; and for "Andy's Christmas Zebra" by Betty Boyles, copyright 1951 by Story Parade, Inc., reprinted by permission.

TONI STRASSMAN—for foreign rights for "Dorrie and the Weather-Box" by Patricia Coombs.

NANCY BYRD TURNER—for her poem "The Romp."

VIKING PRESS, INC.—for "Evening Hymn" from Song in the Meadow by Elizabeth Madox Roberts, copyright 1940 by Elizabeth Madox Roberts, reprinted by permission of the Viking Press, Inc.

HENRY Z. WALCK, INC.—for "Song of the Empty Bottles," by Osmond Molarsky, text copyright ©1968 by Osmond Molarsky, reprinted by permission of Henry Z. Walck, Inc.

FREDERICK WARNE & CO., INC.—for "Oh, Susan Blue" and "Jump-Jump-Jump" by Kate Greenaway, reproduced from Marigold Garden by Kate Greenaway, by permission of Frederick Warne & Co., Inc.

Care has been taken to obtain permission to use copyright material. Any errors are unintentional and will be corrected in future printings if notice is sent to Standard Educational Corporation.

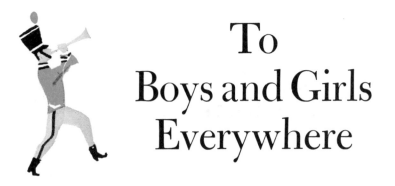

To
Boys and Girls
Everywhere

Boom! Boom! The drums are drumming and the trumpets are blaring and here comes the parade! Do you ever wish there could be a parade every day? We do, and we hope that you do, too. That is why we made this book *Parade of Stories* just for you.

This is a special kind of parade. There are funny circus clowns—but this isn't just a circus parade. There are bears and rabbits and a black cat and his witch — but this isn't just an animal parade or a Halloween parade.

All kinds of creatures are in this parade of stories. Some are as magical as a little boy who came out of a peach. Some are as real as you and your best friend. As they go marching along, you can read their funny stories, exciting stories, all kinds of stories!

Here are rhymes on parade, too — marching rhymes and laughing rhymes, skipping rhymes and rhymes that make you wonder and want to make rhymes of your own.

And all through the parade of stories and rhymes are pictures in wonderful colors—all kinds of pictures!

Do you wish there could be a parade every day? Here it is, for everytime you open the book, the parade will start just for you!

Here comes your very own parade—your *Parade of Stories*.

Contents

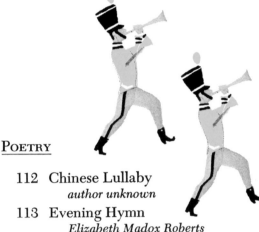

ILLUSTRATION CREDITS

One Cold Day—*Elmer Jacobs*; The Old Woman and Her Pig—*John Faulkner*; Dorrie and the Weather-Box—*Seymour Fleishman*; Pooh Goes Visiting—*Ernest H. Shepard*; Marushka and the Twelve Months—*Joe Rogers*; Momotaro or Little Peach—*George Okomoto*; The Velveteen Rabbit—*Henry Wenclawski*; The Princess and the Pea—*John Faulkner*; Singing—*Dan Siculan*; Oh, Susan Blue—*Dan Siculan*; The Cherry Tree—*Dan Siculan*; Grasshopper Green—*Dan Siculan*; I Like Little Pussy—*Joan Anglund*; The Animal Store—*Robert Christiansen*; The Fairies—*Robert Christiansen*; The Child Next Door—*Eleanore Bowman*; Whistles—*Dan Siculan*; Spring Rain—*Dan Siculan*; Jump-Jump-Jump—*Dan Siculan*; Marching Song—*Dan Siculan*; The Romp—*Joe Pearson*; The Circus Parade—*Elmer Jacobs*; Foreign Lands—*Joe Pearson*; The Day Before April—*Robert Christiansen*; Autumn Woods—*Elmer Jacobs*; Trains—*Dan Siculan*; Ferry Boats—*George Okomoto*; Windy Nights—*Glenn Price*; Mrs. Brown—*Dan Siculan*; Chinese Lullaby—*Dan Siculan*; Evening Hymn—*Elmer Jacobs*; Song of the Empty Bottles—*Dan Siculan*; Yonie Wondernose—*Joe Pearson*; The Sugar Snow—*Eleanore Bowman*; Andy's Christmas Zebra—*Frank C. Murphy*; Sonny-Boy Sim—*George Okomoto*; The Boomer's Fast Sooner Hound—*John Faulkner*

Parade of Stories

ELIZABETH COATSWORTH

One Cold Day

One cold day in late November, when the first snow was beginning to fall, a little boy got lost in the woods.

He hunted east, he hunted west, but he couldn't find his way out. He hunted north, he hunted south, but he couldn't find a little house with a stove in it.

He looked up and he looked down, but he saw only trees, branches and fallen leaves.

So he was very glad when he saw someone in a red overcoat coming through the woods.

9

The someone turned out to be an elderly bear in a fur cap and a muffler and mittens.

"Hello," said the elderly bear. "Lost, eh? Come along with me."

So the little boy went along with the bear, and pretty soon they came to a cave in the rocks. It had a green

door and on the door there was a knocker and a Christ-mas wreath.

The bear opened the door with a latchkey and switched on the lights. Inside, the cave was very cozy. The walls and ceiling were made of uneven rocks, but the floor was smooth and there were several comfortable chairs and a table with a red-and-white cloth. The fire in the stove

crackled merrily, and a pot of chocolate stood at the back keeping warm and there were cinnamon buns in the oven.

The elderly bear and the little boy had a very happy hour, eating and drinking.

In fact the bear asked the little boy if he didn't want to spend the winter with him.

"Of course I snooze a lot in the winter," he explained. "I'll snooze in that chair and you snooze in this one, and we'll have a nice time."

But the little boy wanted to go home and see his folks.

So the bear wrapped up again in his red coat, his fur hat, his muffler and his mittens, and this time he added his overshoes and took the little boy to the edge of the woods and pointed out to him his own house, where the windows had just been lighted.

"Oh, thank you," said the little boy, turning to wave. "Good night."

"He means good-winter, I guess," said the bear good-naturedly to himself as he trudged back into the woods. "Anyway, I mean to sleep all winter!" And he gave a big yawn, and then another.

14

The Old Woman and Her Pig

AN OLD WOMAN was sweeping her house, and she found a little crooked sixpence.

"What," said she, "shall I do with this little sixpence? I will go to market, and buy a little pig."

And so she did.

As she was coming home, she came to a stile.

But the piggy wouldn't go over the stile.

15

She went a little further, and she met a dog.
So she said to him:
 "Dog, dog! Bite pig.
 Piggy won't go over the stile,
 and I shan't get home tonight."
But the dog wouldn't.

She went a little further, and she met a stick.
So she said:
 "Stick! Stick! Beat dog!
 Dog won't bite pig.
 Piggy won't get over the stile,
 and I shan't get home tonight."
But the stick wouldn't.

She went a little further, and she met a fire.
So she said:
 "Fire! Fire! Burn stick!
 Stick won't beat dog.
 Dog won't bite pig.
 Piggy won't get over the stile,
 and I shan't get home tonight."
But the fire wouldn't.

16

She went a little further, and she met some water.
So she said:

> "Water! Water! Quench fire.
> Fire won't burn stick.
> Stick won't beat dog.
> Dog won't bite pig.
> Piggy won't get over the stile,
>   and I shan't get home tonight."

But the water wouldn't.

She went a little further, and she met an ox.
So she said:

> "Ox! Ox! Drink water!
> Water won't quench fire.
> Fire won't burn stick.
> Stick won't beat dog.
> Dog won't bite pig.
> Piggy won't go over the stile,
>   and I shan't get home tonight."

But the ox wouldn't.

She went a little further, and she met a butcher.
So she said:

> "Butcher! Butcher! Kill ox!
> Ox won't drink water.
> Water won't quench fire.
> Fire won't burn stick.
> Stick won't beat dog.
> Dog won't bite pig.
> Piggy won't get over the stile,
>   and I shan't get home tonight."

But the butcher wouldn't.

She went a little further and she met a rope.
So she said:

"Rope! Rope! Hang butcher!
Butcher won't kill ox.
Ox won't drink water.
Water won't quench fire.
Fire won't burn stick.
Stick won't beat dog.
Dog won't bite pig.
Piggy won't get over the stile,
and I shan't get home tonight."
But the rope wouldn't.

She went a little further, and she met a rat.
So she said:

"Rat! Rat! Gnaw rope!
Rope won't hang butcher.
Butcher won't kill ox.
Ox won't drink water.
Water won't quench fire.
Fire won't burn stick.
Stick won't beat dog.
Dog won't bite pig.
Piggy won't get over the stile,
and I shan't get home tonight."
But the rat wouldn't.

18

She went a little further, and she met a cat.
So she said:

> "Cat! Cat! Kill rat!
> Rat won't gnaw rope.
> Rope won't hang butcher.
> Butcher won't kill ox.
> Ox won't drink water.
> Water won't quench fire.
> Fire won't burn stick.
> Stick won't beat dog.
> Dog won't bite pig.
> Piggy won't get over the stile,
> and I shan't get home tonight."

But the cat said to her:

> "If you will go to yonder cow,
> and fetch me a saucer of milk,
> I will kill the rat."

So away went the old woman to the cow.
But the cow said to her:

> "If you will go to yonder haystack,
> and fetch me handful of hay,
> I'll give you the milk."

So away went the old woman to the haystack,
and she brought the hay to the cow.
As soon as the cow had eaten the hay,
she gave the old woman the milk.
So away went the old woman with the milk
in a saucer to the cat.
As soon as the cat had lapped up the milk,
the cat began to kill the rat.

The rat began to gnaw the rope.
The rope began to hang the butcher.
The butcher began to kill the ox.
The ox began to drink the water.
The water began to quench the fire.

The fire began to burn the stick.
The stick began to beat the dog.
The dog began to bite the pig.
The little pig in a fright
jumped over the stile,
and so the old woman
got home that night.

PATRICIA COOMBS

Dorrie and the Weather-Box

THIS IS Dorrie.

She is a witch.

A little witch.

Her room is mixed up, her socks are mixed up, and her hat is always on crooked.

Her mother is the Big Witch.

One Wednesday Dorrie was looking in her closet for her other shoe and she found a picnic basket.

Dorrie looked at the picnic basket. She looked at her black cat, Gink.

"Gink," said Dorrie, "we need a picnic to go in the basket. Maybe Mother and Cook would like to have a picnic, too."

Down,

    down,

        down,

            the stairs

                went Dorrie

                    and Gink went with her.

Dorrie and Gink went into the kitchen. Cook was muttering and kneading bread dough and frowning very hard.

"Cook," said Dorrie, "where is Mother?"

Cook frowned harder and gave the bread dough another whack.

"We're all out of toadstools and she has gone to borrow some from Mr. Obs. They will be back later for tea. I'm busy making bread, so run and play."

"Oh," said Dorrie. "We're going on a picnic. Would you like to go on a picnic with Gink and me?"

Cook stopped whacking the bread and stamped her foot.

"A picnic! It's raining out. Go upstairs and play and don't ask silly questions. I'm busy!"

Dorrie took the picnic basket and went slowly up the stairs. Gink went with her.

"Gink," said Dorrie, "if the clouds went away the rain would stop. If the rain stopped we could go on a picnic."

Gink meowed.

"Shhh!" said Dorrie. "I'm busy thinking."

She looked down the hall at the little door that led to the tower stairs. At the top of the stairs was the secret room where the Big Witch made magic.

Dorrie tiptoed over to the door.

"Hmmm," said Dorrie. "Mother forgot and left the key in the door. I bet she was going to fix the weather before she left and didn't have time. Come on, Gink."

Dorrie opened the door and climbed up the dark stairs. Up and up and up she went and Gink went with her.

Dorrie opened the door to the secret room and went inside. It was dark and spooky and bats flew past her hat. Dorrie shut the door.

Dorrie got out the Big Witch's book of magic and turned the pages.

But she couldn't find any recipes for melting clouds. There was a recipe for cleaning crystal balls, and one for emptying ponds and puddles and filling them up again.

"I bet if I mixed the two together," said Dorrie, "it would work for clouds."

Dorrie got out the bottles and jars and put them beside the cauldron.

"Now, Gink," said Dorrie, "I'll open the window so the clouds can come in here, and I'll find something big with a lid to keep them in."

Dorrie looked around. In a dark corner she saw a big box. She pulled it in front of the window and lifted the lid up.

"There," said Dorrie.

Dorrie began pouring stuff from the bottles and jars into the cauldron. She poured in yellow stuff, and pink stuff, and orange stuff. She dumped in black powder and white powder and stirred it around and around. It began to boil and bubble and glitter, and the smoke curled around and around the room and went out the window. The cauldron bubbled harder and harder. Gink hid under the table beside the picnic basket. Dorrie sang as she stirred:

> Abracadabra blinkety-blue
> Cloud-wish, out-loud wish,
> Wish-away, wish-away, do.

She sang it over and over and over.

The smoke got blacker and blacker and thicker and thicker. The little room got darker and darker.

"Oh my," said Dorrie. She sneezed. Gink sneezed.

The stuff in the cauldron bubbled slowly away.

"This is not a very good recipe," said Dorrie. "It smells awful. But maybe the clouds are going into the box. Let's look, Gink."

Suddenly there was a loud crash of thunder. There was a flash of pink lightning and a flash of yellow lightning. The lightning was shooting out of the box and zigzagging all around the room. The bats squeaked and flapped their wings. Thunder crashed again and the box shook.

"Oh, oh," said Dorrie. "Something is going wrong. That box is too small. The storm is coming out instead of going in."

Dorrie tiptoed over to the box. She pushed the lid down, but it blew off and the lightning zigzagged everywhere. Thunder shook the room and knocked the bottles of magic all over the floor.

Dorrie and Gink ran out of the little room and slammed the door.

Down, down, down the stairs they ran and into the hall.

Dorrie slammed the door to the tower and leaned against it.

"Oh, my," said Dorrie.

A black cloud came through a crack in the door. Orange lightning zigzagged through the keyhole.

The cloud grew bigger and bigger and blacker and blacker.

Dorrie put out her hand. It was raining.

"Oh, Gink," said Dorrie. "We've got the storm *inside* the house. We'll have to try to keep this door shut tight until it clears up."

Dorrie pushed a table and chairs against the door. It was raining harder and harder. Dorrie ran downstairs and got the umbrella and ran upstairs again.

She opened the umbrella and sat down in one of the chairs. Gink sat down beside her.

The clouds were getting thicker and thicker and darker and darker. Rain splashed harder and harder.

Dorrie heard someone shouting. Cook was splashing around the hall, shouting and shaking her fist at the clouds.

"Oh my," said Dorrie. "Cook is awfully cross."

There was a loud crash of thunder and Cook disappeared into the kitchen and slammed the door.

The blackest cloud of all swirled over Dorrie's head, and the wind started whistling through the hall. It blew harder and harder. It blew so hard that the tower door blew open and knocked over the chairs and table. Gink landed in the picnic basket.

"Sit tight, Gink," said Dorrie. The wind lifted them into the air and whirled them around and around and down the stairs.

They sailed into the parlor and out again.

Another gust of wind and a flash of lightning blew open the front door and they sailed right out the door.

Dorrie landed with a thump that knocked Gink out of the basket.

"Ooof," said Dorrie. She looked out from under the umbrella.

"Why, Gink," said Dorrie, "look! The sun is shining!"

There was a shadow beside her. Dorrie looked up. It was the Big Witch and Mr. Obs.

"Oh," said Dorrie. "I'm glad you're home, Mother. Hello, Mr. Obs."

"WHAT have you been doing?" said the Big Witch. "You're soaking wet! And the umbrella is torn and . . ."

A bolt of pink lightning shot out the front door and thunder shook the house.

The Big Witch looked into the hall. Mr. Obs looked, too.

"Amazing!" cried Mr. Obs. "An indoor storm, with pink and yellow and orange lightning. Just like Dorrie's socks."

The Big Witch frowned and looked at Dorrie.

"Dorrie," said the Big Witch, "What did you do while I was gone?"

Dorrie looked at the Big Witch. "I didn't do much of anything, Mother. I found the picnic basket, but it was raining outside so . . ."

"So," said the Big Witch, "you wanted to fix the weather. And as usual, you got into trouble. You not only mixed up my magic, you opened my weather box that says 'DO NOT OPEN.'"

Dorrie looked down at her toes. "I didn't know it was a weather box. It was just a funny box I was going to use to keep the clouds in. A storm came out of it instead."

"It certainly did!" cried Mr. Obs. "Look at the tower!"

The tower was shaking and lightning was shooting out of it in all directions.

The Big Witch grabbed the umbrella and sailed into the house and disappeared up the stairs.

For a few minutes, Dorrie and Gink and Mr. Obs looked through the front door.

Then slowly the lightning and thunder faded away and the clouds changed color.

"Come on in, Mr. Obs," said Dorrie. "Mother has fixed everything."

They stood in the hall and looked at the clouds on the ceiling.

The Big Witch sailed down the stairs with the umbrella.

"Now," she said, "that takes care of that . . ." She stopped and looked up. "Oh my!" said the Big Witch. "Something went wrong!"

It was snowing. It was snowing orange snow faster and faster and faster.

"I love snow!" cried Mr. Obs. "Nice, quiet, orange snow. Come on, Dorrie, we'll make a snowman."

The Big Witch sailed back upstairs with the umbrella.

Dorrie and Mr. Obs made an orange snowman. It looked like Mr. Obs.

Suddenly the air grew brighter and brighter, and warm-er and warmer. The snow stopped and the Big Witch came down the stairs.

The Big Witch looked around.

"Dorrie," she said, "what did you do with Cook?"

"I don't think I turned her into anything," said Dorrie. "She must still be in the kitchen."

They all went into the kitchen. The oven door opened and Cook looked out. She yawned.

"Is the storm over?" she said.

"Yes," said the Big Witch. "And it is time for tea."

Cook climbed out of the oven. She fixed tea and sand-wiches and they all sat around the snowman in the hall and watched it melt.

When the snowman had nearly disappeared, Mr. Obs

took out his violin and
played a tune.

Everybody clapped.

"Mother," said Dorrie,
"I'm sorry I opened the lid
of the weather box and
mixed up the magic."

The Big Witch looked at
Dorrie.

"The next time you plan a
picnic, don't try to change the
weather. And now, go up to
bed. Cook and I will mop up."

Dorrie said good night to
the Big Witch, and to Mr.
Obs, and to Cook, and
climbed up, up, up the stairs.
Gink went with her.

Dorrie put on her night-
gown. She put the picnic basket on the window sill and
looked up at the moon shining
through the clouds.

"Gink," said Dorrie. "I
wish . . . no, maybe I'd better not wish anything more
until tomorrow. I'll just go to
bed and dream I'm a Big
Witch having a picnic on the
moon."

Dorrie fell sound asleep
and so did Gink.

with the original illustrations by
ERNEST H. SHEPARD

A. A. MILNE

Pooh Goes Visiting

(and gets into a tight place)

EDWARD BEAR, known to his friends as Winnie-the-Pooh, or Pooh for short, was walking through the forest one day, humming proudly to himself. He had made up a little hum that very morning, as he was doing his Stoutness Exercises in front of the glass: *Tra-la-la, tra-la-la*, as he stretched up as high as he could go, and then *Tra-la-la, tra-la-oh, help!-la*, as he tried to reach his toes. After breakfast he had said it over and over to himself until he had learnt it off by heart, and now he was humming it right through, properly. It went like this:

> *Tra-la-la, tra-la-la,*
> *Tra-la-la, tra-la-la,*
> *Rum-tum-tiddle-um-tum.*
> *Tiddle-iddle, tiddle-iddle,*
> *Tiddle-iddle, tiddle-iddle,*
> *Rum-tum-tum-tiddle-um.*

Well, he was humming this hum to himself, and walking

along gaily, wondering what everybody else was doing, and what it felt like, being somebody else, when suddenly he came to a sandy bank and in the bank was a large hole.

"Aha!" said Pooh. (*Rum-tum-tiddle-um-tum.*) "If I know anything about anything, that hole means Rabbit," he said, "and Rabbit means Company," he said, "and Company means Food and Listening-to-Me-Humming and such like. *Rum-tum-tum-tiddle-um.*"

So he bent down, put his head into the hole and called out:

"Is anybody at home?"

There was a sudden scuffling noise from inside the hole, and then silence.

"What I said was, 'Is anybody at home?'" called out Pooh very loudly.

"No!" said a voice; and then added, "You needn't shout so loud. I heard you quite well the first time."

"Bother!" said Pooh. "Isn't there anybody here at all?"

"Nobody."

Winnie-the-Pooh took his head out of the hole, and thought for a little, and he thought to himself, "There must be somebody there, because somebody must have *said* 'Nobody.'" So he put his head back in the hole, and said:

"Hallo, Rabbit, isn't that you?"

"No," said Rabbit, in a different sort of voice this time.

"But isn't that Rabbit's voice?"

"I don't *think* so," said Rabbit. "It isn't *meant* to be."

"Oh!" said Pooh.

He took his head out of the hole, and had another think, and then he put it back, and said:

"Well, could you very kindly tell me where Rabbit is?"

"He has gone to see his friend Pooh Bear, who is a great friend of his."

"But this is Me!" said Bear, very much surprised.

"What sort of Me?"

"Pooh Bear."

"Are you sure?" said Rabbit, still more surprised.

"Quite, quite sure," said Pooh.

"Oh, well, then, come in."

So Pooh pushed and pushed and pushed his way through the hole, and at last he got in.

"You were quite right," said Rabbit, looking at him all over. "It *is* you. Glad to see you."

"Who did you think it was?"

"Well, I wasn't sure. You know how it is in the Forest. One can't have *anybody* coming into one's house. One has to be *careful*. What about a mouthful of something?"

Pooh always liked a little something at eleven o'clock in the morning, and he was very glad to see Rabbit getting out the plates and mugs; and when Rabbit said, "Honey or condensed milk with your bread?" he was so excited that he said, "Both," and then, so as not to seem greedy, he added, "But don't bother about the bread, please." And for a long time after that he said nothing . . . until at last, humming to himself in a rather sticky voice, he got up, shook Rabbit lovingly by the paw, and said that he must be going on.

"Must you?" said Rabbit politely.

"Well," said Pooh, "I could stay a little longer if it— if you——" and he tried very hard to look in the direction of the larder.

"As a matter of fact," said Rabbit, "I was going out myself directly."

"Oh, well, then, I'll be going on. Good-bye."

"Well, good-bye, if you're sure you won't have any more."

"*Is* there any more?" asked Pooh quickly.

Rabbit took the covers off the dishes, and said, "No, there wasn't."

"I thought not," said Pooh, nodding to himself. "Well, good-bye. I must be going on."

So he started to climb out of the hole. He pulled with his front paws, and pushed with his back paws, and in a little while his nose was out in the open again . . . and then his shoulders . . . and then—

"Oh, help!" said Pooh. "I'd better go back."

"Oh, bother!" said Pooh. "I shall have to go on."

"I can't do either!" said Pooh. "Oh, help *and* bother!"

Now by this time Rabbit wanted to go for a walk too,

and finding the front door full, he went out by the back door, and came round to Pooh, and looked at him.

"Hallo, are you stuck?" he asked.

"N-no," said Pooh carelessly. "Just resting and thinking and humming to myself."

"Here, give us a paw."

Pooh Bear stretched out a paw, and Rabbit pulled and pulled and pulled . . .

"*Ow!*" cried Pooh. "You're hurting!"

"The fact is," said Rabbit, "You're stuck."

"It all comes," said Pooh crossly, "of not having front doors big enough."

"It all comes," said Rabbit sternly, "of eating too much. I thought at the time," said Rabbit, "only I didn't like to say anything," said Rabbit, "that one of us was eating too much," said Rabbit, "and I knew it wasn't *me*," he said. "Well, well, I shall go and fetch Christopher Robin."

Christopher Robin lived at the other end of the Forest, and when he came back with Rabbit, and saw the front half of Pooh, he said, "Silly old Bear," in such a loving voice that everybody felt quite hopeful again.

"I was just beginning to think," said Bear, sniffing slightly, "that Rabbit might never be able to use his front door again. And I should *hate* that," he said.

"So should I," said Rabbit.

"Use his front door again?" said Christopher Robin. "Of course he'll use his front door again."

"Good," said Rabbit.

"If we can't pull you out, Pooh, we might push you back."

Rabbit scratched his whiskers thoughtfully, and pointed out that, when once Pooh was pushed back, he was back, and of course nobody was more glad to see Pooh than *he* was, still there it was, some lived in trees and some lived underground, and—

"You mean I'd *never* get out?" said Pooh.

"I mean," said Rabbit, "that having got *so* far, it seems a pity to waste it."

Christopher Robin nodded.

"Then there's only one thing to be done," he said. "We shall have to wait for you to get thin again."

"How long does getting thin take?" asked Pooh anxiously.

"About a week, I should think."

"But I can't stay here for a *week!*"

"You can *stay* here all right, silly old Bear. It's getting you out which is so difficult."

"We'll read to you," said Rabbit cheerfully. "And I hope it won't snow," he added. "And I say, old fellow, you're taking up a good deal of room in my house—do you mind if I use your back legs as a towel-horse? Because, I mean, there they are—doing nothing—and it would be very convenient just to hang the towels on them."

"A week!" said Pooh gloomily. "*What about meals?*"

"I'm afraid no meals," said Christopher Robin, "because of getting thin quicker. But we will *read* to you."

Bear began to sigh, and then found he couldn't because he was so tightly stuck; and a tear rolled down his eye, as he said:

"Then would you read a Sustaining Book, such as would

help and comfort a Wedged Bear in Great Tightness?"

So for a week Christopher Robin read that sort of book at the North end of Pooh,

and Rabbit

hung his washing on the South end . . . and in between Bear felt himself getting slenderer and slenderer. And at the end of the week Christopher Robin said, *"Now!"*

So he took hold of Pooh's
front paws and Rabbit took
hold of Christopher Robin,
and all Rabbit's friends and
relations took hold of Rabbit, and they all pulled together.

And for a long time Pooh
only said, "*Ow!*" . . .

And "Oh!" . . .

And then, all of a sudden,
he said "*Pop!*" just as if a

cork were coming out of a bottle.

And Christopher Robin and Rabbit and all Rabbit's friends and relations went head-over-heels backwards . . . and on the top of them came Winnie-the-Pooh—free!

So, with a nod of thanks to his friends, he went on with his walk through the forest, humming proudly to himself. But, Christopher Robin looked after him lovingly, and said to himself, "Silly old Bear!"

Marushka
and the
Twelve Months

ONCE UPON A TIME a woman and her two daughters lived in a little house beside a steep mountain. The woman loved the older girl dearly, for Holena was her own daughter. The younger girl, Marushka, was gentle and good, but her stepmother never had a kind word for her.

Holena did nothing all day long but dress up in her best clothes and look in the mirror to see if her hair curled or her nose looked less pointed.

Marushka worked hard all day long. She cooked and baked. She washed and scrubbed. She fed the pigs and

46

milked the cow. But the harder she worked, the more her stepmother scolded and often Marushka was sent to bed hungry.

Yet she was so sweet and good that she never complained, and the older she grew, the sweeter and prettier she grew. Her stepmother and sister became more and more jealous.

"Soon it will be time for the young men to come courting," thought her stepmother. "Who will look at my Holena when Marushka is near?"

"This mirror is old," Holena thought angrily. "It does not show me clearly. I *know* I am prettier than Marushka!"

But Marushka was far prettier than Holena, and Holena knew it.

So the stepmother and Holena decided they must drive Marushka away.

One cold winter day Holena called Marushka to her.

"Go up the mountain," she ordered sharply, "and get me some violets. And they must be fresh and sweet. Hurry!"

"But, sister," said Marushka, bewildered. "How can I find violets in winter? They do not bloom in the snow."

"Don't answer me back!" shouted Holena. "Go and bring me sweet violets. And do not come back without them."

The stepmother added her

harsh orders, and the two pushed Marushka out of the house and slammed the door behind her.

Weeping, Marushka began to climb up the mountain. All around the snow lay white and deep. With each step, she sank into it. There was no sign anywhere of another living being, man or animal.

Shivering with cold in her thin dress, she wandered for a long time until she was lost. She was almost ready to give up when, far ahead, she saw a glowing light.

So she struggled on, up and up the steep mountain. At the very top, she came to a clearing. And there was a great fire. Around the fire were twelve stones and on the stones sat twelve men in white robes.

Three of the men were very old. Three were not quite so old. Three were middle-aged men, and the three youngest were tall, handsome boys. The oldest man had a long white beard and long, flowing white hair. He sat on a stone that was higher than the other stones. This was the great January, and the twelve men were the twelve Months.

The twelve men did not speak. They sat silently, looking at the glowing fire.

At first Marushka was too frightened to move. Then timidly she stepped toward the fire.

"Kind sirs," she said politely, "may I warm myself at your fire? I am so cold!"

The great January raised his head and looked at her.

"This is no place for you, my child," he said in his deep, kind voice. Why are you here?"

"I am looking for violets," said Marushka.

"This is not the time for violets," said January. "They do not bloom in the snow."

"I know," said Marushka sadly, "but my sister Holena sent me. She told me I must bring her fresh, sweet violets and not to come back without them. My stepmother said that, too. Please, sir, will you tell me where to find violets?"

January picked up a long staff that lay at his feet. He arose and walked over to one of the youngest Months, and put the staff in his hand.

"Brother March," he said. "Take the high seat."

March went to the high seat and waved the staff over the fire. At once the fire blazed up to the sky and the snow began to melt. The trees began to bud. Green grass sprang up and in the grass pink daisies and yellow primroses flowered. It was spring!

As Marusha watched, violets began to peep out from among the leaves until the ground was blue with them.

"Gather your violets quickly, Marushka," said March.

Joyfully Marushka gathered the fragrant blue flowers until she had filled her arms.

"Thank you! Oh, thank you!" she cried to the twelve Months and then she hastened down the mountain.

How surprised Holena and the stepmother were when the door of the the little house flew open and there stood Marushka with her arms filled with blue violets!

Their fragrance filled the little house with sweetness and Holena snatched them without a word of thanks.

"Where did you find the violets?" she demanded.

"Up, up on the mountain," said Marushka. "The ground was covered with them."

Holena made a wreath of violets to wear on her hair and the stepmother fastened a clump of violets to her dress, but they did not let Marushka even come close to the flowers to smell them.

And the next day Holena called Marushka to her.

"Go up the mountain," she ordered sharply, "and get me some strawberries. I am hungry for their taste so make sure they are ripe and sweet. Hurry!"

"But, sister," protested Marushka, "how can I find strawberries in winter? They do not ripen in the snow."

"Don't answer me back!" shouted Holena. "Go and bring me ripe strawberries. And don't come back without them."

And again she and the stepmother pushed Marushka out of the house and slammed the door behind her.

How cold the wind blew! Shivering in her thin dress, Marushka began to climb up the mountain again. The snow lay white and deep and with every step she sank into it. At last, just when she thought she could not take another step, she saw the fire, far ahead, again.

Eagerly, she climbed toward it.

The twelve Months sat silently around the great, glowing fire, just as they had the day before. Again January sat on the highest stone.

Marushka stepped toward the fire.

"Kind sirs," she said politely. "May I warm myself at your fire? I am so cold!"

Great January raised his head and nodded.

"Marushka," he said. "Why have you come again?"

"I am looking for strawberries," said Marushka.

"But, child," said January. "This is not the time for strawberries. They do not ripen in the snow."

"I know," said Marushka sadly, "but my sister Holena sent me. She told me I must bring her ripe, sweet strawberries and not to come back without them. My stepmother said so, too. Please, sir, will you tell me where to find strawberries?"

Great January picked up the staff that lay at his feet. He stood up and walked over to the Month that sat opposite him.

"Brother June," he said, giving him the staff. "Take the high seat."

June went to the high seat and waved the staff over the fire. At once the fire blazed to the sky, and the snow melted.

In an instant, the grass was green, leaves rustled on the trees, birds sang sweetly, and flowers blossomed in the forest. It was summer!

As Marushka watched, starry blossoms appeared under the beech trees. Swiftly they changed to fruit that was first green, then pink, then red. The ground was covered with ripe, red strawberries!

"Gather your strawberries quickly, Marushka," said June.

Joyfully Marushka picked the ripe, red strawberries until her apron was full of them.

"Thank you, oh, thank you, kind sirs!" she cried to the twelve Months and hastened down the mountain.

How surprised Holena and the stepmother were when the door of the little house flew open and there stood Marushka with her apron full of the ripe, red berries!

The fragrance of the wild strawberries filled the house. Holena snatched them without a word of thanks.

"Where did you find the strawberries?" she demanded.

"Up, up on the mountain," said Marushka. "The ground was covered with them."

Holena ate and ate the strawberries until her mouth and fingers were stained with the sweet, red juice. Her mother ate all the strawberries she wanted, too.

But not one strawberry was given to Marushka. Not once did the stepmother or Holena say,

"Here is a juicy berry for you, Marushka."

In a day or two, the strawberries were all gone. Then Holena called Marushka to her.

"Go up the mountain," she ordered sharply, "and get me some apples. And make sure they are big and sweet and red. Hurry!"

"But, sister," protested Marushka, "how can I find apples in winter? The trees are bare. They have neither leaves nor fruit on them now."

"Don't answer me back!" shouted Holena. "Go and bring me red apples. And don't come back without them."

As before, the stepmother added her harsh orders, and the two pushed Marushka out of the house and slammed the door behind her.

The snow was falling thickly as Marushka again began the climb up the mountain. Again and again she lost her way, but at last, far ahead, she saw the glow of the fire.

There were the twelve Months still seated around the great fire on their stones. Great January still sat on the highest stone. In silence, they looked at the fire.

Marushka stepped forward.

"Kind sirs," she said politely. "May I warm myself at your fire? I am so cold!"

Great January raised his head.

"Child," he said, "Why have you come again?"

"I am looking for red apples," said Marushka.

"But, Marushka," said January. "This is not the time for apples. The trees are bare."

"I know," said Marushka unhappily, "but my sister Holena sent me. I must bring her back red apples or I cannot go home. My stepmother said so, too. Please, sir, will you tell me where to find apples?"

Great January picked up the staff that lay at his feet. Slowly he stood up and walked over to one of the older Months. He gave the staff to him.

"Brother September," he said. "Take the high seat."

September went to the high seat and waved the staff over the fire. Red flames burned and glowed and the snow

melted away. The grass was yellow and dry. On the trees, leaves appeared and changed quickly to brilliant scarlet and gold. A wind blew coldly and the leaves began to fall and scatter.

Then Marushka saw an apple tree, on which hung big, red apples.

"Gather your apples quickly, little Marushka," said the kind September.

Marushka ran to the tree and shook it. A ripe red apple

fell down. Then another big red apple tumbled into her reaching hands.

"That is enough," said September. "Don't pick any more, Marushka."

At once Marushka moved away from the apple tree. With the two red apples in her hands, she cried,

"Oh, thank you! Thank you, kind sirs!" And she turned and hastened happily down the mountain.

As she came up to the door of the little house, it flew open and Holena and the stepmother stared at the apples in her hands. They were so astonished, they did not speak a word.

"See, sister!" said Marushka joyfully. "Here are your red apples. See how big and ripe they are!"

Holena snatched the apples from her.

"Where did you find the apples?" she demanded.

"Up, up on the mountain," said Marushka. "There were many hanging on the apple tree."

"Many!" said Holena. "You brought only two. Did you stop and eat all the rest yourself, wicked girl?"

"No, no, sister," protested Marushka. "I did not take one taste of an apple. When I shook the tree, only two apples fell down. Then they told me to stop, so I did and came straight home."

Holena would not believe her.

"I'll shake you like an apple tree!" she shouted and the stepmother scolded and scolded until Marushka covered her ears with her hands and ran away to the kitchen.

Then Holena took a bite of one apple and her mother took a bite of the other apple and the apples were so delicious, they ate them down to the cores. Never had they tasted apples like these, and they both had a longing for more.

"Mother," said Holena. "She said many apples were hanging from the apple tree. Get me my warm cloak with the hood and I will go up the mountain myself. And when I find that apple tree, I will shake and shake until all the apples fall down. No one will make me stop!"

Her mother did not want Holena to go up the steep, snowy mountain.

"Let us send Marushka again," she said. "She can bring us more apples."

"No," said Holena. "She will eat them all herself. I will go."

And no matter how her mother begged and pleaded, she would not listen. At last, her mother let her have her way. She brought the warm cloak and helped Holena into it. She fastened the hood snugly on Holena's head.

Then Holena began to climb up the steep mountain while her mother stood in the open doorway and watched.

All around the snow lay white and deep. There was no sign of another living being on the mountain. Even in her

warm cloak and hood, Holena shivered, but she was stubborn. She wanted those red apples, and she would find
them.

At last she saw the glow of the great fire and when she
came up to it, there were the twelve Months seated on
their stones around it. Great January still sat on the highest stone with his staff at his feet.

Holena was frightened at first, but then she pushed
through the circle of seated men without a "Please" or
"May I?" She held her hands over the fire to warm them.

Great January raised his head.

"Who are you?" he asked in his deep voice. "What do
you want?"

"Why should I tell you?" Holena asked rudely. "It is
no business of yours, old man!"

Great January frowned, and suddenly the sky was black
with storm clouds. He waved his staff over the fire, and

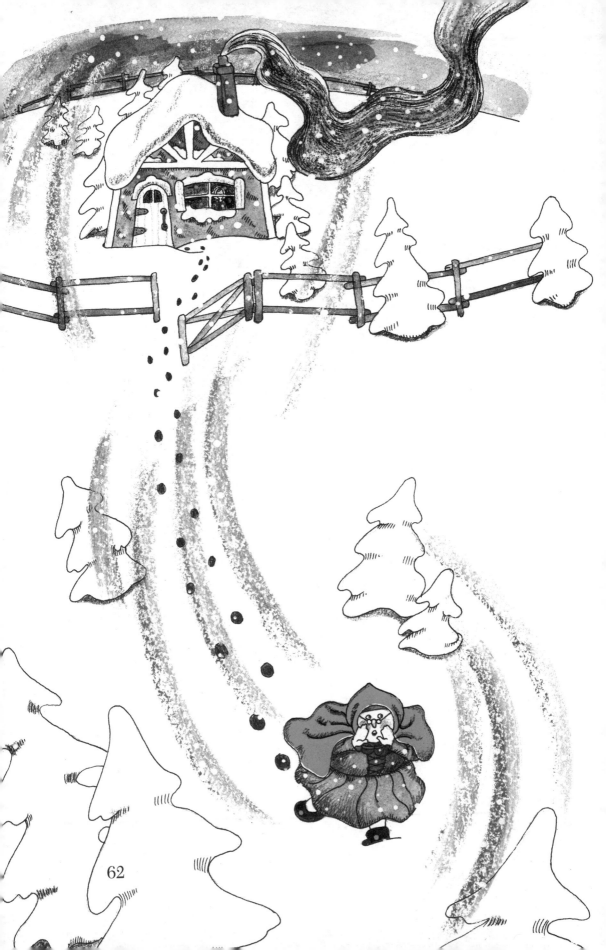

the red flames flickered and died. A fierce wind howled and snow began falling, thick and fast. The fire and the twelve Months disappeared. Holena was alone on the mountain in a wild snowstorm.

She forgot all about the red apples. All she wanted to do was go home. So she plunged down the mountain, but the snow fell so fast and thick, she could not find her way. She was lost in a blowing white wilderness.

Meanwhile in the little house, her mother waited and waited. She ran from the window to the doorway, trying to see if Holena were coming, but Holena did not come. The hours passed slowly.

"Where can she be?" she thought in terror. "Did the apples put a spell on her so she can't leave them? I must go and find her."

So at last she put on her own warm cloak and hood and struggled up the mountain. But the snow blew and blew, white and thick, covering everything, and so, she, too, was lost.

"Holena!" she called. "Holena!" But there was no answer.

In the little house, Marushka waited for them anxiously. She kept the fire on the hearth glowing so the house would be warm when they came home. But they did not come that night. They did not come in the morning. They never came back again.

Little Marushka lived on in the small house beside the mountain. Now the house and the cow and the pigs belonged to her. And after a time a handsome and good young farmer came to court her. They were married and lived together happily in the little house all their lives long.

Momotaro

OR LITTLE PEACH

A LONG, LONG TIME AGO there lived an old man and an
old woman in the country of Japan. The old couple were
very sad and lonely because they had no children. One
day the old man went to the mountains to cut wood, and
the old woman went to the river to wash clothes. While
the old woman was washing the clothes a great something
came tumbling and splashing down the river. Grabbing a
piece of bamboo that lay nearby, she pulled it to her.
When she took it up and looked at it, she saw that it was a

64

very large peach. It was the biggest peach she had ever seen. She then quickly finished her washing and returned home to give the peach to the old man to eat.

When the time came for their supper the old woman took a big knife to cut the peach in half. As she was about to use the knife a voice from inside the peach said "Wait! Don't cut me!" Immediately after that, the peach split open and out jumped a beautiful boy baby. Great was the surprise and joy of the old couple to see the child. They took him for their own son and named him Momotaro, which means Little Peach, because he came out of a peach.

The old man and the old woman loved Momotaro and took great care of him. So the boy grew up strong and brave and in time wanted to do something to help his country. Now in a distant part of the sea there was an

island called the Island of the Ogres. Upon it lived the ogres who sailed the seven seas in search of riches. So powerful and so wicked were these robber-ogres that no country was safe from them.

One day Momotaro said to the old man and the old woman, "I should like to go to the land of the wicked ogres, and bring back the treasures which they have taken from our land. Would it please you to have me do this?"

Momotaro's words made the old couple very happy. It made them very happy, too, that their son wanted to help his country. The old man gave Little Peach a sword and a suit of armor for his journey. The old woman made him some millet dumplings. Then Momotaro set out for the Island of the Ogres, promising the old couple that he would soon return.

As Momotaro was walking toward the sea he met a dog. The dog growled and said, "Momotaro, what have you there hanging from your belt?"

"I have some of the very best Japanese millet dumplings," replied Momotaro.

"Give me one and I will go with you," said the dog.

So Momotaro took a dumpling out of his pouch and gave it to the dog.

As Momotaro and the dog kept on walking toward the sea they met a monkey. The monkey made a face at the

66

dog and said, "Momotaro, what have you there hanging from your belt?"

"I have some of the very best Japanese millet dumplings," replied Momotaro.

"Give me one and I will go with you," said the monkey.

So Momotaro took a dumpling out of his pouch and gave it to the monkey.

As Momotaro and the dog and the monkey kept on

walking toward the sea they met a pheasant. The pheasant dragged a wing on the ground and said with a gay nod of his brilliantly-colored head, "Momotaro, what have you hanging from your belt?"

"I have some of the very best Japanese millet dumplings in the pouch that hangs from my belt," replied Momotaro.

"Give me one and I will go with you," said the pheasant.

So Momotaro took a dumpling out of his pouch and gave it to the pheasant.

With Momotaro at their head the dog and the monkey and the pheasant, who usually hated each other, became good friends and faithfully followed their leader to the sea. There, at the edge of the sea, Momotaro built a boat. Then he and the dog and the monkey and the pheasant set sail for the Island of the Ogres.

In no time they arrived at the island and at once broke through the front gate. There they met many of the follow-

ers of the chief of the ogres who tried to fight them. But Momotaro and the three who went along with him were too much for them. The pheasant pecked at the heads and faces of the wicked ogres. The monkey clawed at them. The dog bit them. And Momotaro shook his sword threateningly at them. At last, they met the chief.

Then came the real battle. The chief hit at Momotaro with an iron club, but Momotaro was ready for him and so dodged every blow directed at him. When the chief saw that he could not hit Momotaro he rushed forward to wrestle with him. Without difficulty Momotaro just crushed down the chief ogre and held him so tightly that he could not move. All this was done in a fair fight.

After this the ogres promised never to do wicked things

again, and the chief said he would give up his treasures. "Out with your riches then!" said Momotaro. Then the chief and his followers took from their huge treasure chests great stores of gold and silver and precious jewels and placed them before Momotaro. Little Peach and his three helpers carried all these riches onto their boat and set sail for home.

The old man and the old woman were very glad and very thankful, too, when Little Peach was safely home. As for Momotaro, he gave great feasts to which all the people, rich and poor, were invited. He told them many stories of his adventures and never forgot to praise the dog and the monkey and the pheasant for their help. Without them, he said, he never could have won over the bad ogres so soon and so easily.

Momotaro became very rich and a very honorable man. He shared his riches with the old man and the old woman, and so they all lived happily ever after.

MARGERY W. BIANCO

The Velveteen Rabbit

THERE WAS ONCE a velveteen rabbit, and in the beginning he was really splendid. He was fat and bunchy, as a rabbit should be; his coat was spotted brown and white, he had real thread whiskers, and his ears were lined with pink sateen. On Christmas morning, when he sat wedged in the top of the Boy's stocking, with a sprig of holly between his paws, the effect was charming.

There were other things in the stocking, nuts and oranges and a toy engine, and chocolate almonds and a clockwork mouse, but the Rabbit was quite the best of all. For at least two hours the Boy loved him, and then Aunts and Uncles came to dinner, and there was a great rustling of tissue paper and unwrapping of parcels, and in the excitement of looking at all the new presents the Velveteen Rabbit was forgotten.

For a long time he lived in the toy cupboard or on the nursery floor, and no one thought very much about him. He was naturally shy, and being only made of velveteen, some of the more expensive toys quite snubbed him.

The mechanical toys were very superior, and looked down upon every one else; they were full of modern ideas, and pretended they were real. The model boat, who had lived through two seasons and lost most of his paint, caught the tone from them and never missed an opportunity of referring to his rigging in technical terms. The Rabbit could not claim to be a model of anything, for he didn't know that real rabbits existed; he thought they were all stuffed with sawdust like himself, and he understood that sawdust was quite out-of-date and should never be mentioned in modern circles. Even Timothy, the jointed wooden lion, who was made by the disabled soldiers, and should have had broader views, put on airs and pretended he was connected with Government. Between them all the poor little Rabbit was made to feel himself very insignificant and commonplace, and the only person who was kind to him at all was the Skin Horse.

The Skin Horse had lived longer in the nursery than

any of the others. He was so old that his brown coat was bald in patches and showed the seams underneath, and most of the hairs in his tail had been pulled out to string bead necklaces. He was wise, for he had seen a long succession of mechanical toys arrive to boast and swagger, and by-and-by break their mainsprings and pass away, and he knew that they were only toys, and would never turn into anything else. For nursery magic is very strange and wonderful, and only those playthings that are old and wise and experienced like the Skin Horse understand all about it.

"What is REAL?" asked the Rabbit one day, when they were lying side by side near the nursery fender, before Nana came to tidy the room. "Does it mean having things that buzz inside you and a stick-out handle?"

"Real isn't how you are made," said the Skin Horse. "It's a thing that happens to you. When a child loves you for a long, long time, not just to play with, but REALLY loves you, then you become Real."

"Does it hurt?" asked the Rabbit.

"Sometimes," said the Skin Horse, for he was always truthful. "When you are Real you don't mind being hurt."

"Does it happen all at once, like being wound up," he asked, "or bit by bit?"

"It doesn't happen all at once," said the Skin Horse. "You become. It takes a long time. That's why it doesn't often happen to people who break easily, or have sharp edges, or who have to be carefully kept. Generally, by the time you are Real, most of your hair has been loved off, and your eyes drop out and you get loose in the joints and very shabby. But these thing don't matter at all, because once you are Real you can't be ugly, except to people who don't understand."

"I suppose you are Real?" said the Rabbit. And then he wished he had not said it, for he thought the Skin Horse might be sensitive. But the Skin Horse only smiled.

"The Boy's Uncle made me Real," he said. "That was a great many years ago; but once you are Real you can't become unreal again. It lasts always."

The Rabbit sighed. He thought it would be a long time before this magic called Real happened to him. He longed to become Real, to know what it felt.like; and yet the idea of growing shabby and losing his eyes and whiskers was rather sad. He wished that he could become it without these uncomfortable things happening to him.

There was a person called Nana who ruled the nursery. Sometimes she took no notice of the playthings lying about, and sometimes, for no reason whatever, she went swooping about and hustled them away in cupboards. She called this "tidying up," and the playthings all hated it, especially the tin ones. The Rabbit didn't mind it so much, for wherever he was thrown he came down soft.

One evening, when the Boy was going to bed, he couldn't find the china dog that always slept with him. Nana was in a hurry, and it was too much trouble to hunt for china dogs at bedtime, so she simply looked about her, and seeing that the toy cupboard door stood open, she made a swoop.

"Here," she said, "take your old Bunny! He'll go to sleep with you!" And she dragged the Rabbit out by one ear, and put him into the Boy's arms.

That night, and for many nights after, the Velveteen
Rabbit slept in the Boy's bed. At first he found it rather
uncomfortable, for the Boy hugged him very tight, and
sometimes he rolled over on him, and sometimes he
pushed him so far under the pillow that the Rabbit could
scarcely breathe. And he missed, too, those long moonlight hours in the nursery, when all the house was silent,
and his talks with the Skin Horse. But very soon he grew
to like it, for the Boy used to talk to him, and made nice
tunnels for him under the bed-clothes that he said were
like the burrows the real rabbits lived in. And they had
splendid games together, in whispers when Nana had gone
away to her supper and left the night-light burning on
the mantelpiece. And when the Boy dropped off to sleep,
the Rabbit would snuggle down close under his little warm
chin and dream, with the Boy's hands clasped close round
him all night long.

And so time went on, and the little Rabbit was very
happy—so happy that he never noticed how his beautiful velveteen fur was getting shabbier and shabbier, and

his tail coming unsewn, and all the pink rubbed off his nose where the Boy had kissed him.

Spring came, and they had long days in the garden, for wherever the Boy went the Rabbit went too. He had rides in the wheelbarrow, and picnics on the grass, and lovely fairy huts built for him under the raspberry canes behind the flower border. And once, when the Boy was called away suddenly to go out to tea, the Rabbit was left out on the lawn until long after dusk, and Nana had to come and look for him with the candle because the Boy couldn't go to sleep unless he was there. He was wet through with the dew and quite earthy from diving into the burrows the Boy had made for him in the flower bed, and Nana grumbled as she rubbed him off with a corner of her apron.

"You must have your old Bunny!" she said. "Fancy all that fuss for a toy!"

The boy sat up in bed and stretched out his hands.

"Give me my Bunny!" he said. "You mustn't say that. He isn't a toy. He's REAL!"

When the little Rabbit heard that he was happy, for he knew that what the Skin Horse had said was true at last. The nursery magic had happened to him, and he was a toy no longer. He was REAL. The Boy himself had said it.

That night he was almost too happy to sleep, and so much love stirred in his little sawdust heart that it almost burst. And into his boot-button eyes, that had long ago lost their polish, there came a look of wisdom and beauty, so that even Nana noticed it next morning when she picked him up, and said, "I declare if that old Bunny hasn't got quite a knowing expression!"

That was a wonderful Summer!

Near the house where they lived there was a wood, and in the long June evenings the Boy liked to go there after tea to play. He took the Velveteen Rabbit with him, and before he wandered off to pick flowers, or play at brigands among the trees, he always made the Rabbit a little nest somewhere among the bracken, where he would be quite cozy, for he was a kind-hearted little boy and he liked Bunny to be comfortable. One evening, while the Rabbit was lying there alone, watching the ants that ran to and fro between his velvet paws in the grass, he saw two strange beings creep out of the tall bracken near him.

They were rabbits like himself, but quite furry and brand-new. They must have been very well made, for their seams didn't show at all, and they changed shape in a queer way when they moved; one minute they were long and thin and the next minute fat and bunchy, instead of always staying the same like he did. Their feet padded softly on the ground, and they crept quite close to him, twitching their noses, while the Rabbit stared hard to see which side the clockwork stuck out, for he knew that people who jump generally have something to wind them up. But he couldn't see it. They were evidently a new kind of rabbit altogether.

They stared at him, and the little Rabbit stared back. And all the time their noses twitched.

"Why don't you get up and play with us?" one of them asked.

"I don't feel like it," said the Rabbit, for he didn't want to explain that he had no clockwork.

"Ho!" said the furry rabbit. "It's as easy as anything." And he gave a big hop sideways and stood on his hind legs.

"I don't believe you can!" he said.

"I can!" said the little Rabbit. "I can jump higher than anything!" He meant when the Boy threw him, but of course he didn't want to say so.

"Can you hop on your hind legs?" asked the furry rabbit.

That was a dreadful question, for the Velveteen Rabbit had no hind legs at all! The back of him was made all in one piece, like a pincushion. He sat still in the bracken, and hoped that the other rabbits wouldn't notice.

"I don't want to!" he said again.

But the wild rabbits have very sharp eyes. And this one stretched out his neck and looked.

"He hasn't got any hind legs!" he called out. "Fancy a rabbit without any hind legs!" And he began to laugh.

"I have!" cried the little Rabbit. "I have got hind legs! I am sitting on them!"

"Then stretch them out and show me, like this!" said the wild rabbit. And he began to whirl round and dance, till the little Rabbit got quite dizzy.

"I don't like dancing," he said. "I'd rather sit still!"

But all the while he was longing to dance, for a funny new tickly feeling ran through him, and he felt he would give anything in the world to be able to jump about like these rabbits did.

The strange rabbit stopped dancing, and came quite close. He came so close this time that his long whiskers brushed the Velveteen Rabbit's ear, and then he wrinkled his nose suddenly and flattened his ears and jumped backwards.

"He doesn't smell right!" he exclaimed. "He isn't a rabbit at all! He isn't real!"

"I am Real!" said the little Rabbit. "I am Real! The Boy said so!" And he nearly began to cry.

Just then there was a sound of footsteps, and the Boy ran past near them, and with a stamp of feet and a flash of white tails the two strange rabbits disappeared.

"Come back and play with me!" called the little Rabbit. "Oh, do come back! I know I am Real!"

But there was no answer, only the little ants ran to and fro, and the bracken swayed gently where the two strangers had passed. The Velveteen Rabbit was all alone.

"Oh, dear!" he thought. "Why did they run away like that? Why couldn't they stop and talk to me?"

For a long time he lay very still, watching the bracken, and hoping that they would come back. But they never returned and presently the sun sank lower and the little white moths fluttered out, and the Boy came and carried him home.

Weeks passed, and the little Rabbit grew very old and shabby, but the Boy loved him just as much. He loved him so hard that he loved all his whiskers off, and the pink lining to his ears turned grey, and his brown spots faded. He even began to lose his shape, and he scarcely looked like a rabbit any more. except to the Boy. To him he was always beautiful, and that was all that the little Rabbit cared about. He didn't mind how he looked to other peo-

78

ple, because the nursery magic had made him Real, and when you are Real, shabbiness doesn't matter.

And then, one day, the Boy was ill.

His face grew very flushed, and he talked in his sleep, and his little body was so hot that it burned the Rabbit when he held him close. Strange people came and went in the nursery, and a light burned all night, and through it all the little Velveteen Rabbit lay there, hidden from sight under the bedclothes, and he never stirred, for he was afraid that if they found him some one might take him away, and he knew that the Boy needed him.

It was a long weary time, for the Boy was too ill to play, and the little Rabbit found it rather dull with nothing to do all day long. But he snuggled down patiently, and looked forward to the time when the Boy should be well again, and they would go out in the garden amongst the flowers and the butterflies and play splendid games in the raspberry thicket like they used to. All sorts of delightful things he planned, and while the Boy lay half asleep he crept up close to the pillow and whispered them in his ear. And presently the fever turned, and the Boy got better. He was able to sit up in bed and look at picture books, while the little Rabbit cuddled close at his side. And one day, they let him get up and dress.

It was a bright, sunny morning, and the windows stood wide open. They had carried the Boy out on to the balcony, wrapped in a shawl, and the little Rabbit lay tangled up among the bedclothes, thinking.

The Boy was going to the seaside tomorrow. Everything was arranged, and now it only remained to carry out the doctor's orders. They talked about it all, while the little Rabbit lay under the bedclothes, with just his head peeping out, and listened. The room was to be disinfected, and all the books and toys that the Boy had played with in bed must be burnt.

"Hurrah!" thought the little Rabbit. "Tomorrow we shall go to the seaside," and he wanted very much to see the big waves coming in, and the tiny crabs, and the sand castles.

Just then Nana caught sight of him.

"How about his old Bunny?" she asked.

"That?" said the doctor. "Why, it's a mass of scarlet fever germs!—Burn it at once. What? Nonsense! Get him a new one. He mustn't have that any more!"

And so the little Rabbit was put into a sack with the old picture-books and a lot of rubbish, and carried out to the end of the garden behind the fowl-house. That was a fine place to make a bonfire, only the gardener was too busy just then to attend to it. He had the potatoes to dig

80

and the green peas to gather, but next morning he promised to come quite early and burn the whole lot.

That night the Boy slept in a different bedroom, and he
had a new bunny to sleep with him. It was a splendid
bunny, all white plush with real glass eyes, but the Boy
was too excited to care very much about it. For to-morrow
he was going to the seaside, and that in itself was such a
wonderful thing that he could think of nothing else.

And while the Boy was asleep, dreaming of the seaside, the little Rabbit lay among the old picture-books in
the corner behind the fowl-house, and he felt very lonely.
The sack had been left untied, and so by wriggling a bit
he was able to get his head through the opening and look
out.

He was shivering a little, for he had always been used to sleeping in a proper bed, and by this time his coat had worn so thin and threadbare from hugging that it was no longer any protection to him. Near by he could see the thicket of raspberry canes, growing tall and close like a tropical jungle, in whose shadow he had played with the Boy on bygone mornings.

He thought of those long sunlit hours in the garden—how happy they were—and a great sadness came over him.

He seemed to see them all pass before him, each more beautiful, than the other, the fairy huts in the flower-bed, the quite evenings in the wood when he lay in the bracken and the little ants ran over his paws; the wonderful day when he first knew that he was Real. He thought of the Skin Horse, so wise and gentle, and all that he had told him. Of what use was it to be loved and lose one's beauty and become Real if it all ended like this? And a tear, a real tear, trickled down his little shabby velvet nose and fell to the ground.

And then a strange thing happened. For where the tear had fallen a flower grew out of the ground, a mysterious flower, not at all like any that grew in the garden. It had slender green leaves the colour of emeralds, and in the centre of the leaves a blossom like a golden cup. It was so beautiful that the little Rabbit forgot to cry, and just lay there watching it. And presently the blossom opened, and out of it there stepped a fairy.

She was quite the loveliest fairy in the whole world. Her dress was of pearl and dewdrops, and there were flowers round her neck and in her hair, and her face was like the most perfect flower of all. And she came close to the little

Rabbit and gathered him up in her arms and kissed him on his velveteen nose that was all damp from crying.

"Little Rabbit," she said, "don't you know who I am?"

The Rabbit looked up at her, and it seemed to him that he had seen her face before, but he couldn't think where.

"I am the nursery magic Fairy," she said. "I take care of all the playthings that the children have loved. When they are old and worn out and the children don't need them any more, then I come and take them away with me and turn them into Real."

"Wasn't I Real before?" asked the little Rabbit.

"You were Real to the Boy," the Fairy said, "because he loved you. Now you shall be Real to every one."

And she held the little Rabbit close in her arms and flew with him into the wood.

It was light now, for the moon had risen. All the forest was beautiful, and the fronds of the bracken shone like frosted silver. In the open glade between the tree-trunks the wild rabbits danced with their shadows on the velvet grass, but when they saw the Fairy they all stopped dancing and stood round in a ring to stare at her.

"I've brought you a new playfellow," the Fairy said. "You must be very kind to him and teach him all he needs to know in Rabbitland, for he is going to live with you for ever and ever!"

And she kissed the little Rabbit again and put him down on the grass.

"Run and play, little Rabbit!" she said.

But the little Rabbit sat quite still for a moment and never moved. For when he saw all the wild rabbits dancing around him he suddenly remembered about his hind legs, and he didn't want them to see that he was made all in one piece. He did not know that when the Fairy kissed him that last time she had changed him altogether. And he might have sat there a long time, too shy to move, if just then something hadn't tickled his nose, and before he thought what he was doing he lifted his hind toe to scratch it.

And he found that he actually had hind legs! Instead of dingy velveteen he had brown fur, soft and shiny, his ears twitched by themselves, and his whiskers were so long that they brushed the grass. He gave one leap and the joy of using those hind legs was so great that he went springing about the turf on them, jumping sideways and whirling round as the others did, and he grew so excited that when at last he did stop to look for the Fairy she had gone.

He was a Real Rabbit at last, at home with the other rabbits.

Autumn passed and Winter, and in the Spring, when the days grew warm and sunny, the Boy went out to play in the wood behind the house. And while he was playing, two rabbits crept out from the bracken and peeped at him. One of them was brown all over, but the other had strange markings under his fur, as though long ago he had been spotted, and the spots still showed through. And about his little soft nose and his round black eyes there was something familiar, so that the Boy thought to himself:

"Why, he looks just like my old Bunny that was lost when I had scarlet fever!"

But he never knew that it really was his own Bunny, come back to look at the child who had first helped him to be Real.

HANS CHRISTIAN ANDERSEN

The Princess and the Pea

ONCE UPON A TIME there was a prince who wanted to marry a princess, but she must be a *real* princess. So he traveled all around the world to find one.

There were plenty of princesses. As he traveled near and far, the prince saw many lovely princesses, but whether they were real princesses or not, he could not tell. Always there seemed to be something just a little wrong.

So, sadly, the prince came home again. He was very unhappy because he had set his heart on finding a real princess.

One evening there was a terrible storm. It thundered and it lightened and the rain poured down in torrents. Truly it was a fearful night.

All at once there was a knock at the palace gate and the old king himself went to open it.

There outside stood a princess, but what a sight she was from the rain and the storm! Water streamed out of her hair and her clothes. Water ran in at the toes of her shoes and out at the heels. Yet she said she was a real princess.

"Well, we shall soon find out if that is true," thought the old queen, but she said nothing.

Instead she went into the bedchamber, pulled all the bedclothes off, and placed a single pea on the bed boards.

Then she took twenty mattresses and piled them on top of the pea. And then she piled twenty feather beds, stuffed with eiderdown, on top of the mattresses.

When that was done, she

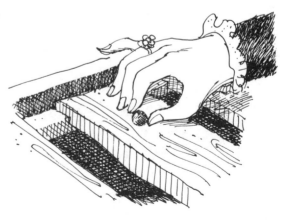

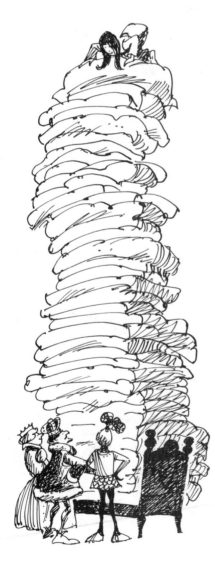

led the princess into the bed-chamber and helped her climb up, up, up to the top of the feather beds. That was where the princess was to sleep that night.

In the morning they asked her how she had slept.

"Oh, badly!" she said. "I hardly closed my eyes all the night long. I don't know what could have been in the bed, but I was lying upon something so hard that my whole body is black and blue. It was truly dreadful!"

Then they knew she must be a real princess because she had felt the pea through the twenty mattresses and twenty feather beds. No one but a real princess could have such a delicate skin.

So the happy prince took her to be his wife, for now he was sure he had found a real princess.

And the pea was put into a velvet-lined glass box in the royal museum where it still may be seen—unless somebody has eaten it. ■

Poetry

Singing

Of speckled eggs the birdie sings
    And nests among the trees;
The sailor sings of ropes and things
    In ships upon the seas.

The children sing in far Japan.
    The children sing in Spain;
The organ with the organ man
    Is singing in the rain.

            —Robert Louis Stevenson

89

The Cherry Tree

Mother shake the cherry tree.
Susan catch a cherry;
Oh how funny that will be,
Let's be merry!

—*Christina Rossetti*

Oh, Susan Blue

Oh, Susan Blue,
How do you do?
Please may I go for a walk
with you?
Where shall we go?
Oh, I know—
Down in the meadow where
the cowslips grow!

—*Kate Greenaway*

Grasshopper Green

Grasshopper green is a comical chap; ·
    He lives on the best of fare.
Bright little trousers, jacket, and cap,
    These are his summer wear.
Out in the meadow he loves to go,
    Playing away in the sun;
It's hopperty, skipperty, high and low,
    Summer's the time for fun.

Grasshopper green has a quaint little house;
    It's under the hedge so gay.
Grandmother Spider, as still as a mouse,
    Watches him over the way.
Gladly he's calling the children, I know,
    Out in the beautiful sun;
It's hopperty, skipperty, high and low,
    Summer's the time for fun.

—Traditional

I Like Little Pussy

I like little pussy,
    Her coat is so warm;
And if I don't hurt her
    She'll do me no harm.
So I'll not pull her tail,
    Nor drive her away,
But Pussy and I
    Very gently will play;
She shall sit by my side,
    And I'll give her some food;
And she'll love me because
    I am gentle and good.

I'll pat little Pussy,
    And then she will purr,
And thus show her thanks
    For my kindness to her;
I'll not pinch her ears,
    Nor tread on her paw,
Lest I should provoke her
    To use her sharp claw;
I never will vex her,
    Nor make her displeased,
For Pussy can't bear
    To be worried or teased.

—*Jane Taylor*

The Animal Store

If I had a hundred dollars to spend,
    Or maybe a little more,
I'd hurry as fast as my legs would go
    Straight to the animal store.

I wouldn't say, "How much for this or that?"—
    "What kind of a dog is he?"
I'd buy as many as rolled an eye,
    Or wagged a tail at me!

I'd take the hound with the drooping ears
    That sits by himself alone;
Cockers and Cairns and wobbly pups
    For to be my very own.

I might buy a parrot all red and green,
    And the monkey I saw before,
If I had a hundred dollars to spend,
    Or maybe a little more.

—*Rachel Field*

The Fairies

Up the airy mountain,
   Down the rushy glen,
We daren't go a-hunting
   For fear of little men;
Wee folk, good folk,
   Trooping all together;
Green jacket, red cap,
   And white owl's feather!

Down along the rocky shore
  Some make their home;
They live on crispy pancakes
  Of yellow tide-foam;
Some in the reeds
  Of the black mountain lake,
With frogs for their watch-dogs
  All night awake.

High on the hilltop
  The old King sits;
He is now so old and gray
  He's nigh lost his wits.
With a bridge of white mist
  Columbkill he crosses,
On his stately journeys
  From Slieveleague to Rosses;
Or going up with music
  On cold starry nights,
To sup with the Queen
  Of the gay Northern Lights.

They stole little Bridget
  For seven years long;
When she came down again
  Her friends were all gone.
They took her lightly back
  Between the night and morrow;
They thought that she was fast asleep,
  But she was dead with sorrow.
They have kept her ever since
  Deep within the lake,
On a bed of flag-leaves,
  Watching till she wake.

By the craggy hillside,
  Through the mosses bare,
They have planted thorn-trees
  For pleasure here and there.
Is any man so daring
  As dig them up in spite,
He shall find their sharpest thorns
  In his bed at night.

Up the airy mountain,
  Down the rushy glen,
We daren't go a-hunting
  For fear of little men;
Wee folk, good folk,
  Trooping all together;
Green jacket, red cap,
  And white owl's feather!

—*William Allingham*

95

The Child Next Door

The child next door has a wreath on her hat,
Her afternoon frock sticks out like that,
    All soft and frilly;
She doesn't believe in fairies at all
(She told me over the garden wall)—
    She thinks they're silly.

The child next door has a watch of her own,
She has shiny hair and her name is Joan,
    (Mine's only Mary);
But doesn't it seem very sad to you
To think that she never her whole life through
    Has seen a fairy?

—*Rose Fyleman*

96

Whistles

I want to learn to whistle.
I've always wanted to.
I fix my mouth to do it but
The whistle won't come through.

I think perhaps it's stuck, and so
I try it once again.
Can people swallow whistles?
Where is my whistle then?

—*Dorothy Aldis*

Spring Rain

The storm came up so very quick
   It couldn't have been quicker.
I should have brought my hat along,
   I should have brought my slicker.

My hair is wet, my feet are wet,
   I couldn't be much wetter.
I fell into a river once
   But this is even better.

—*Marchette Chute*

Jump, Jump, Jump

Jump—jump—jump—
   Jump away
From this town into
   The next, to-day.

Jump—jump—jump—
   Jump over the moon;
Jump all the morning,
   And all the noon.

Jump—jump—jump—
   Jump all night;
Won't our mothers
   Be in a fright?

Jump—jump—jump—
   Over the sea;
What wonderful wonders
   We shall see.

Jump—jump—jump—
   Jump far away;
And all come home
   Some other day.

—*Kate Greenaway*

Marching Song

Bring the comb and play upon it!
  Marching, here we come!
Willie cocks his highland bonnet,
  Johnnie beats the drum.

Mary Jane commands the party,
  Peter leads the rear;
Feet in time, alert and hearty,
  Each a Grenadier!

All in the most martial manner
  Marching double-quick;
While the napkin, like a banner,
  Waves upon the stick!

Here's enough of fame and pillage,
  Great commander Jane!
Now that we've been round the village,
  Let's go home again.

—*Robert Louis Stevenson*

The Romp

The wind came dashing from the wood
    With sudden roars and rushes,
Leapfrogging over little hills
    And tagging all the bushes.

It rollicked through the countryside,
    It capered through the town,
It blew one kite into the sky
    And blew another down.

Young Lucy Ann was off to school.
    In vain she whimpered, "Stop!"
It had that girl with skirts a-twirl
    And spinning like a top.

The parson had a tall black hat;
    He tipped it to the people.
Wind caught it as he went along
    And tossed it to the steeple.

Good Mrs. Brown was hanging clothes.
   Calm little frocks and breeches
Began to hop upon the line
   Like frisky imps and witches.

The wind was wild; it couldn't seem
   To get its fill of fun.
It puffed, "I'm in a perfect gale!"
   Then roared about the pun.

Skylarking, leaping, on it went,
   Till old man Weather said,
"There, silly wind, you'll lose your breath.
   Go home and go to bed."

So, panting hard, it hurried home
   And weary went to bed.
"What lovely games we had today,
   The world and I!" it said.

—*Nancy Byrd Turner*

JOE PEARSON

The Circus Parade

O Goody, it's coming, the circus parade
    And all the way up the street,
What crowds of people in gay-colored clothes,
    With popcorn and peanuts to eat!

The children have red, blue, and yellow bal-
    loons,
    As up by the curbing they stand,
And now, in the distance, we suddenly hear
    The circus's big brass band!

Behind the crash-bang! of the music they play,
    Come riders in red velvet gowns,
And after them doing the funniest things,
    A silly procession of clowns.

Then lions and tigers that pace up and down,
    In wagons all painted with gold,
And monkeys a-playing just all kinds of tricks,
    As they grimace and chatter and scold.

O, next there come camels and elephants, too,
    High on their backs men ride;
There are queer little ponies, no bigger than
    dogs,
    With a clown on a donkey, beside!

And then there come chariots rumbling by
    With horses all four in a row;
And the wheezing, old, piping calliope is
    The very tail end of the show!

—*Olive Beaupré Miller*

Elmer Jacobs

103

Foreign Lands

Up into the cherry tree
Who should climb but little me?
I held the trunk with both my hands
And looked abroad on foreign lands.

I saw the next door garden lie,
Adorned with flowers before my eye,
And many pleasant places more
That I had never seen before.

104

I saw the dimpling river pass
And be the sky's blue looking-glass;
The dusty roads go up and down,
With people tramping in to town.

If I could find a higher tree,
Farther and farther I should see,
To where the grown-up river slips
Into the sea among the ships,

To where the roads on either hand
Lead onward into fairy land,
Where all the children dine at five,
And all the playthings come alive.

—*Robert Louis Stevenson*

The Day Before April

The day before April
    Alone, alone,
I walked in the woods
    And I sat on a stone.

I sat on a broad stone
    And sang to the birds.
The tune was God's making
    But I made the words.

—*Mary Carolyn Davies*

Autumn Woods

I like the woods
    In autumn
When dry leaves hide the ground,
When the trees are bare
And the wind sweeps by
With a lonesome rushing sound.

I can rustle the leaves
    In autumn
And I can make a bed
In the thick dry leaves
That have fallen
From the bare trees
    Overhead.

—*James S. Tippett*

Trains

Over the mountains,
Over the plains,
Over the rivers,
Here come the trains.

Carrying passengers,
Carrying mail,
Bringing their precious loads
In without fail.

Thousands of freight cars
All rushing on
Through day and darkness,
Through dusk and dawn.

Over the mountains,
Over the plains,
Over the rivers,
Here come the trains.

—*James S. Tippett*

Ferry Boats

Over the river,
Over the bay,
Ferry-boats travel
Every day.

Most of the people
Crowd to the side
Just to enjoy
Their ferry-boat ride.

Watching the seagulls,
Laughing with friends,
I'm always sorry
When the ride ends.

—James S. Tippett

OKAMOTO

Windy Nights

Whenever the moon and stars are set,
Whenever the wind is high,
All night long in the dark and wet,
A man goes riding by.
Late in the night when the fires are out,
Why does he gallop and gallop about?

Whenever the trees are crying aloud,
And ships are tossed at sea,
By, on the highway, low and loud,
By at the gallop goes he:
By at the gallop he goes, and then
By he comes back at the gallop again.

—*Robert Louis Stevenson*

Mrs. Brown

As soon as I'm in bed at night
And snugly settled down,
The little girl I am by day
Goes very suddenly away,
And then I'm Mrs. Brown.

I have a family of six,
And all of them have names,
The girls are Joyce and Nancy Maud,
The boys are Marmaduke and Claude
And Percival and James.

We have a house with twenty rooms
A mile away from town;
I think it's good for girls and boys
To be allowed to make a noise—
And so does Mr. Brown.

We do the most exciting things,
Enough to make you creep;
And on and on and on we go—
I sometimes wonder if I know
When I have gone to sleep.

—*Rose Fyleman*

Chinese Lullaby

Chinese Sandmen,
Old and wise,
With soft dream-songs
Close our eyes.
And queen of all their lullabies
Is a maid with almond eyes.
On her ancient moon-guitar
She strums a sleep-song to a star;
And when big China-shadows fall
Snow-white lilies hear her call.
Chinese Sandmen,
Old and wise,
With soft dream-songs
Close our eyes.

—*Author Unknown*

Evening Hymn

The day is done;
The lamps are lit;
Woods-ward the birds are flown.
Shadows draw close,—
Peace be unto this house.

The cloth is fair;
The food is set.
God's night draws near.
Quiet and love and peace
Be to this, our rest, our place.

—*Elizabeth Madox Roberts*

OSMOND MOLARSKY

Song of the Empty Bottles

THADDEUS WENT to the Neighborhood House after school whenever he felt like it—to make pictures with crayons or finger paints, play ping-pong and have fun. Some days he felt like it, and some days he did not. But he never missed going on Thursday, because on that afternoon Mr. Andrews came to sing songs with his guitar.

Some of the songs were happy and some were sad, and the children all sang along with Mr. Andrews—all but Thaddeus, who made his mouth go but did not sing out loud because he would rather listen. He did not want to miss hearing one single boom of Mr. Andrews' deep voice or a single pling-plung of his guitar. Instead, he waited until he was alone. Then he sang the songs, by himself.

Sometimes when he was singing, Thaddeus thought of songs that he had never heard before.

> My mamma goes away all day,
> My mamma goes away all day,
> My mamma goes away all day.

114

Then Thaddeus wished, more than he wished for anything else in the world, that he had a guitar, to make the wonderful pling-plung sounds to go along with his singing, the way Mr. Andrews did.

One day when all the children were crowded around, Mr. Andrews said, "The boy in the back there. I don't think I know your name."

The other children looked around at Thaddeus and Thaddeus looked behind him, to see who Mr. Andrews was talking to.

"No. I mean you, young fellow. Come inside the circle. I want to talk to you." He was looking right at Thaddeus. "That's right. Come here."

Thaddeus felt hot and cold and frightened. He loved Mr. Andrews, but he had never dared go up and talk to him and lean against him, as some of the others did. But now the circle opened in front of him, and slowly he came near.

"What is your name?" Mr. Andrews asked.

Thaddeus put his head down and said in a soft voice, "Thaddeus."

"I didn't quite hear that," Mr. Andrews said.

"Thaddeus!" the other children screamed. "His name is Thaddeus!"

"I want to hear it from this young man himself," and Mr. Andrews put his arm around Thaddeus' shoulders.

Then Thaddeus spoke right up and said, "Thaddeus."

"Now will you tell me why you make believe you are singing in the back there, when you're really not singing at all?"

"I like to hear you sing," Thaddeus said. "And if I sing, then I can't hear you."

Mr. Andrews looked surprised and tried not to smile. "Well, I am flattered," he said. "But you would have fun singing along with the others, if you tried it."

"I have fun hearing. I sing when I'm by myself."

The other children were beginning to drift away, and after a while only Thaddeus was there with Mr. Andrews. Suddenly he reached out and touched the strings of Mr. Andrews' guitar.

"Here, hold it," Mr. Andrews said, and he put the guitar in Thaddeus' arms in just the right way. Thaddeus drew his thumb across the strings four times. Each time he could feel the whole guitar tremble in his arms, and he could hear the strings ring in his ears like a million bells.

He said very softly, "How much is a guitar?"

"This one cost a great deal of money. A hundred dollars. Why do you want to know?"

"I want to have a guitar," Thaddeus said.

"But you don't know how to play one."

"I could learn."

Mr. Andrews looked hard at Thaddeus. At last he said, "I just happen to know someone who has a very nice guitar that he will sell for fifteen dollars. Do you suppose you could get fifteen dollars to buy it with?"

"I don't know" Thaddeus said, and he got up and walked quickly out of the Neighborhood House, straight up the hill and home, where he waited for his mother to come from work.

"What have you got inside you?" his little sister Bernadine asked. Even when Thaddeus was only sitting quietly on the front steps, his sister always could tell when he had something on his mind.

"Nothing much," Thaddeus said.

"Tell me."

"I want to buy a guitar," he said.

"Will you let me play it?"

"Sometimes, if you're very careful."

"I'll be careful," Bernadine said.

After a while their mother came up the hill and turned in at the little iron gate. She sat down on the front steps to catch her breath.

"Have you children been good today?"

"Yes," Bernadine said. "Thaddeus wants to buy a guitar."

"A guitar! What do you want with a guitar?"

"I want to play it and sing with it."

"That's for big kids. You're too small to play a guitar."

118

"Can he?" Bernadine asked, following her mother into the house.

"Can he what?"

"Can he get a guitar?"

"How much is a guitar?"

"A hundred dollars," Thaddeus said.

"Are you out of your mind, boy?"

"But I can get one for fifteen dollars."

"Oh, that's different," his mother said. "No problem at all. You just go out in the yard and water the little banty tree every day for a week, and it will start growing dollar bills and quarters and dimes and nickles. Then you can pick them off and go downtown and buy anything you like. And while you're down there, would you mind buying me a dress and some shoes?"

Thaddeus knew that this was his mother's way of saying

they did not have fifteen dollars for a guitar. Not right now. Or any other time, for that matter.

The next Thursday, after the story and singing time, Thaddeus waited to talk to Mr. Andrews. He told him how much he still wanted the guitar.

"Did you ever think of trying to earn some money?" Mr. Andrews asked.

"How could I earn some money?"

"Oh, I don't know. Running errands. Doing chores for people in your neighborhood."

"People in my neighborhood don't have any more money than my mamma," Thaddeus said. "They do their own chores and run their own errands."

"Yes," said Mr. Andrews. "Of course."

"I do earn money sometimes," Thaddeus said. "But only a little bit. Enough to buy an ice cream cone or a bottle of soda."

"How do you earn that money?"

"I collect empty bottles and take them back to the store. I collect old newspapers and take them to the shredding factory. They pay ten cents for a whole wagon-load."

"Do you have a wagon?"

"An old rickety wagon," said Thaddeus.

"Well, if you collect enough wagonloads of old news-papers and find enough bottles, and if you don't spend the money for things to eat but save it all up, pretty soon you'll have enough to buy your guitar."

"How soon?"

"If you start right away, maybe you can earn the money by the Fourth of July—that's about three months."

"I wish it was July right now," said Thaddeus.

"Then you wouldn't have anything to look forward to."

"I would have the guitar."

"You win," said Mr. Andrews. "In the meantime, I'll teach you a little about how to play the guitar. We can use mine."

Mr. Andrews showed Thaddeus how to rest the guitar on his lap, with the fingers of his left hand pressing down on the strings and the fingers of his right hand plunking them. At first the strings cut into his fingers and hurt, and it was hard to remember where to put his fingers to get the sound he wanted. Often he made mistakes, and harsh sounds came from the strings. But he kept on trying, and every week, after the other children went home, Mr. Andrews gave him a lesson.

In time, Thaddeus learned six different ways to put his fingers down on the strings, to make six different chords. Each chord sounded different from all the others, and he loved every one of them. And no matter what note he sang, he could always find a chord on the guitar that made his song sound beautiful.

More than ever Thaddeus found himself making up songs, as he practiced on Mr. Andrews' guitar.

It's a hot day, Mr. Fireman.
Please open the fire hydrant for us.
It's a hot day, Mr. Fireman.
Please open the fire hydrant for us.

"That's a nice song," Mr. Andrews said when Thaddeus sang it. "Maybe someday you'll make up a longer one."

Thaddeus thought about that for a while. Then he said, "Yes, maybe I will."

Not as much fun as learning to play the guitar was collecting bottles and newspapers. No matter where he went, Thaddeus kept his eyes open for empty bottles. He found them in alleys and beside park benches. It was hard, slow work, and often he felt very discouraged.

But then Thaddeus discovered the tall apartment buildings that began a few blocks from his house. He heard

122

that the people who lived in these buildings left their empty bottles in incinerator closets on every floor. They left old newspapers there too. He asked the building superintendents if he could have the bottles and newspapers. Some said he couldn't, but some said he could. With his rickety wagon he carted the bottles to the grocery store, where he got refund money for them. He took the newspapers to the paper-shredding factory on the street behind his house. He collected every day after school and on Saturdays and Sundays, and he saved all the money he earned. He kept it in a peanut butter jar and didn't tell anyone about it, not even Bernadine.

Every few days, Thaddeus dumped his money out on his bed to see how much he had. The pile of nickles and dimes grew very slowly, and after eight weeks he only had four dollars and seventy-one cents—it would take him forever to save fifteen dollars. But then he thought about the guitar, and he put the money back in the peanut butter jar and went out again to find more bottles and newspapers.

One Sunday afternoon he went, as usual, to the Oxford House, which was ten stories tall. Every Sunday, for the past eight weeks, he had taken the elevator to the tenth floor and looked in the closet. He would look in the closet on every floor, right down to the ground. He did the same thing in all the houses in the neighborhood.

This Sunday afternoon, the doorman at the Oxford House wouldn't let him in. "Can't have you in the building," he said.

Thaddeus left and went to the Cambridge House. The same thing happened there. "No boys allowed inside," the doorman said. "Go away."

It was the same at the Eaton House, the Rugby House, the Wiltshire Apartments and the Hampshire House. "Go away. No boys allowed." That was the story everywhere.

At the Embassy Gardens the doorman said, "Sorry, young fellow. Can't let you in."

"Why not?"

"There've been some robberies around here."

"Oh," said Thaddeus. "But I'm not a robber."

"I know you're not. All the same, those are my orders. Sorry." Then a lady came out and the doorman blew his whistle for a taxi, and Thaddeus went away.

The next Thursday, Thaddeus went to the Neighborhood House. At the end of the singing, he started to leave with the others, but Mr. Andrews stopped him. "Aren't you going to take your lesson today?"

"I don't feel like it," Thaddeus said.

"Why not?" said Mr. Andrews. "What's the matter?"

"Nothing much."

"Come on, now. Tell me. I want to know."

So Thaddeus said, "I can't get any more bottles from the apartment houses. They won't let me in. Now I don't think I can ever find enough bottles to save up fifteen dollars."

Mr. Andrews didn't say anything. He just strummed quietly on his guitar, and Thaddeus could see that he was thinking. Finally he said, "You don't care very much about collecting empty bottles, do you?"

"No, I don't care much about it at all."

"What do you like to do?" Mr. Andrews asked

"I like to make songs and sing them."

"That's what I thought. But you've never really made up a whole song, have you? Like 'Blue Tail Fly' or 'Oh! Susanna.'"

"I guess not," said Thaddeus.

"Why don't you try?" said Mr. Andrews. "Whenever I hear a new song, I write it down. Then I can save it and sing it whenever I want to. Here's what I'll do. If you make up a song that I like, I'll pay you ten dollars for it. Then you will have enough money to buy the guitar and have a few dollars left over. Is that a bargain?"

Thaddeus could hardly believe it. Ten dollars for a song! It would take five hundred bottles to get ten dollars. And a ton of newspapers to get nine dollars.

A song was something you couldn't see or touch. How could it be worth ten dollars?

Well, if Mr. Andrews said so, then it must be so. Thaddeus walked home thinking that he would make up a song that very night, after he went to bed.

Up until now, whenever Thaddeus made up a song, he did it without trying. It just came to him. He might be walking down the street and see something and make up a song about it. But, when he went to bed and tried to make up a song, no song came.

No matter how hard Thaddeus tried—day or night, walking, running, standing still or lying down—no new song came to him. What he thought, at first, was going to be a quick way of earning ten dollars was turning out to be very hard. Maybe collecting bottles was an easier way, after all.

And so, once again, he began to keep a sharp lookout for bottles. He had only collected a few when he suddenly realized that he was singing, making up a new song—a song about empty bottles. The words and the tune came to him in bits and pieces.

The first time was when he saw three bottles high on a wall. He had to wait for a tall boy to come along and get them down for him. "I saw three bottles on a

high wall. I wished that I was six feet tall." Thaddeus thought maybe he could put that in a song.

Another time, he put nine bottles on the kitchen table and tapped them with a spoon. Each bottle made a different sound, and Thaddeus discovered that he could play a tune on them. This gave him an idea for still another verse. "I tapped some bottles with my spoon and got this funny little tune." Making up a song wasn't so hard, after all.

Then he remembered that the songs Mr. Andrews sang had a chorus that came after every verse. What could the chorus be? Thaddeus thought, "I can even find bottles in the dark," and then he thought, "That could be the chorus. 'Bottles in the alley, bottles in the park. If there is a bottle, I can find it in the dark.'"

As Thaddeus continued to look for bottles, he thought of more verses for his song. Some were good, and he re-

127

membered them and put them in. Others he decided were not as good, and he just forgot them.

At last, he thought that his song was long enough. When Thursday came, he took his money jar and went to the Neighborhood House. After the other children had gone, Thaddeus picked up Mr. Andrews' guitar and sang his song and played chords to go with it, to make his voice bounce and float along, high and sweet.

> *I look for bottles ev'rywhere,*
> *Where I find them I don't care.*
>
> *Bottles in the alley, bottles in the park,*
> *If there is a bottle, I can find it in the dark.*
>
> *I saw three bottles on a high wall,*
> *I wished that I was six feet tall.*
>
> *Bottles in the alley, bottles in the park,*
> *If there is a bottle, I can find it in the dark.*
>
> *I tapped some bottles with my spoon*
> *And got this funny little tune.*
>
> *Bottles in the alley, bottles in the park,*
> *If there is a bottle, I can find it in the dark.*
>
> *I saw a bottle in the lake,*
> *Reached it with a big, long rake.*
>
> *Bottles in the alley, bottles in the park,*
> *If there is a bottle, I can find it in the dark.*

After the first time, Mr. Andrews sang along with him on the chorus. Thaddeus could tell that Mr. Andrews liked the song, and he was not surprised. He liked the song himself.

Then Mr. Andrews asked Thaddeus to sing it again. He took out a pad and pencil and wrote down the words and drew some lines and marked down some notes. "All it needs now is a name," Mr. Andrews said. "What do you think of calling it 'The Empty Bottle Song'?"

"I like that fine," Thaddeus said, and Mr. Andrews wrote it down.

"Thank you for the song," Mr. Andrews said. Then he took ten one-dollar bills out of his wallet and handed them to Thaddeus.

"Just a minute. The guitar is in my car," Mr. Andrews said, and he went outside.

Thaddeus emptied his jar of money on a chair, counted out five dollars and put it with the ten Mr. Andrews had given him.

Now Mr. Andrews brought the guitar in, handling it with great care, and polished it up a little with his handkerchief. Thaddeus could hardly wait to hold it. "Here's the fifteen dollars," he said.

"Thank you," said Mr. Andrews. "Here is your guitar,"

and he handed it to Thaddeus. How cool and smooth it felt, and it shone like a mirror. And when Thaddeus drew his right thumb softly across the strings, the guitar trembled. It was smaller and lighter than Mr. Andrews' guitar but just the right size for a boy. It did not have such a loud voice either, but it had a sweet voice. Thaddeus thought it was the sweetest sound he had ever heard.

Thaddeus carried his guitar home more carefully than he would carry half a dozen eggs. He walked fast but he didn't run, and he picked his feet up at curbs so he wouldn't trip. There, at last, was the iron gate to his yard, the scrawny little banty tree, the front stoop, the front door.

Thaddeus set his guitar down on the kitchen table. He got a glass of water and drank it, then got another and went out and poured it on the banty tree. How did he know? Maybe the poor little thing was thirsty.

Then he sat down on the front porch with his guitar and began to sing and play. He played "Blue Tail Fly," and he played "Oh! Susanna" and he played "Go Down Moses."

Pretty soon, people sitting in their windows and on their stoops across the street were singing along with him.

When Bernadine came home, she stopped outside the gate for just a minute, then came in and sat down next to her brother.

It was getting close to six o'clock. Any minute now, their mother would be coming up the hill from work, out of breath and tired. Thaddeus was playing a song the neighbors didn't know, but they were catching on when he sang the chorus.

> *Bottles in the alley, bottles in the park,*
> *If there is a bottle, I can find it in the dark.*

Thaddeus was singing a verse of the song as his mother reached the gate. She stood there listening.

> *I saw a bottle in the lake,*
> *Reached it with a big, long rake.*

Then everybody joined in.

> *Bottles in the alley, bottles in the park,*
> *If there is a bottle, I can find it in the dark.*

That was the end of the song, and Thaddeus' mother came through the gate.

"What are we going to have for supper?" said Thaddeus.

"Son, I see you got that guitar, after all."

"Yes, Mamma."

"Where'd you get all that money to buy it?"

Thaddeus almost said, "I picked it off the little banty tree, Mamma." But he didn't say it. He said, "Some of it I earned collecting bottles and papers. And some of it Mr. Andrews paid me for making up a song."

"Well, all I can say is, you're going to come to a good end or a bad end. I don't know which. You mark my words. Now you go right on singing. I'll listen from inside. I'm going to fix some supper."

Thaddeus drew his thumb over the strings three times and began to sing again. But this time it was a brand-new song. He had begun to smell the dinner his mother was cooking, and it was making him very hungry—so hungry that his new song was all about food.

Pancakes, cornflakes, squash and cherries,
Pickles, lemons, beans and berries.

This is the food I love to eat.
I don't care if it's sour or sweet.

Grapes and apples, bread and honey,
Stew and chicken, chocolate money.

This is the food I love to eat.
I don't care if it's sour or sweet.

His mother was calling him now. After dinner, he would make up more words for the new song. Then he could sing it for Mr. Andrews on Thursday.

MARGUERITE DE ANGELI

Yonie Wondernose

YONIE WAS a little Pennsylvania Dutch boy. He was seven. He lived with Mom and Pop, Malinda, Lydia, and little Nancy on a farm in Lancaster County. His brother Ammon was grown up and had been away for a long time. Granny lived on the farm, too. She lived in her own part of the house. But most of the time she was in the kitchen helping Mom and Malinda.

Yonie's real name was Jonathan, but everyone called him Yonie. Pop called him "Yonie Wondernose" because he was so curious. He wanted to know about everything. If Pop brought a package into the house, he must see what was in it. If the Bishop came to talk to Pop, he must listen. If Mom had a pot boiling on the stove, he must lift the lid to see what was cooking. Sometimes the steam burned his nose, but didn't keep him from looking the next time. If Malinda was baking a cake, Yonie was sure to open the oven door to see what kind it was.

"A Wondernose you are for sure!" she would scold. "Look now how it falls so fast!"

When Yonie and Lydia were on their way to school, he stopped so many times that they were often late.

He hung over the fence to watch the men filling the wagons with stones from the stone crusher. He stood watching while a man changed a tire on a car, or while Nathan Straub seeded the bean field.

"We'll be late!" wailed Lydia. "Come now!"

But she stood to watch, too!

Yonie's jacket was fastened with hooks and eyes instead of buttons. Pop didn't have buttons on his suit either. That is because he was an Amishman. And the Amish people never use buttons unless they are necessary. Yonie wore a broad hat just like Pop's hat, too—a straw one in summer and a black felt one in winter. And Mom cut Yonie's hair around a bowl, just like she cut Pop's. But Pop wore a beard such as all Amishmen wear.

This afternoon Pop and Mom were going visiting.

They were taking Malinda and Lydia with them in the Germantown wagon, and they would stay overnight. Granny, Yonie, and Nancy stood in the doorway to see them off.

"Good-bye," said Pop. "Don't be a Wondernose, now, and forget what you are doing!"

"No, Pop, I won't," Yonie answered.

"Remember, you are the man of the house now," said Mom.

"Ya, I will," Yonie nodded and stood straighter.

"Take good care of the barn creatures," called Pop again. "Feed and water them well. Don't forget, if anything happens, be sure to look after the horses first. They get scared so fast. Next, look after Dunder, the red bull. He cost a lot of money, so take good care of him, don't forget! We see, now, if you are a man!"

Then he winked, and Yonie knew what he meant. Pop had promised him something when he was old enough to be trusted like a man but no one, not even Mom, knew about that promise. It was a secret between Pop and Yonie.

"I won't forget!" he called back.

As the wagon drove off, he thought, "Now Pop thinks I'll be a Wondernose, but I'll show him how big and smart I can be! When he comes home tomorrow, he'll see that I can take care of the animals by myself. Then, maybe, he'll let me do what he promised!"

"Ya, vell," said Granny. "Soon it makes time for supper. More round-wood I need for the fire, and the cistern water iss all! The last I used for sprinkling the plants and for scrubbing."

Cistern water was soft rain water that Granny liked best for washing dishes and such things.

Pop teased Granny because she was always scrubbing.

"It's a wonder you don't scrub the hoe handles and the

fence posts, you are so clean!" he would say.

But Granny only said, "Better so, as like some I know, with floors all smeary and things all hoddled up!" and went on scrubbing.

Yonie knew he must pump a lot of water to keep Granny supplied. He must get the wood for the kitchen stove. But he must take care of the animals, too.

He went first to the pasture for the cows, Blossom, Bluebell, and Buttercup. As they ambled down the lane, a squirrel scolded at Yonie from the fence rail, then scampered up a tree and into a knothole. Yonie *must* see where he went. Up the tree he scrambled and peered into the hole. He thrust his finger in to see what he could find. But he drew it out again in a hurry, for Mr. Squirrel gave it a sharp bite!

"Ach!" Yonie scolded himself, "here I am, being a Wondernose, just like always."

When he climbed down from the tree, the cows had scattered to nibble the grass at the edges of the lane. It took Yonie some time to get them started again in the right direction and to their places in the cowshed. He hurried to throw down fresh straw for their beds, while Granny milked. He carried water for them and called Nancy to come and put milk in the cats' dish for Malta and the four kittens.

He took the horses to the trough for water. He patted

Star's broad back and thought of what Pop had promised. Then he went to look after Dunder. Dunder was kept in a pen and shed of his own on the far side of the barn.

Yonie had helped Pop, but he had never taken care of Dunder by himself as Ammon always had. He knew he must speak quietly to the great beast. He knew how to use the staff that Pop kept handy, too, and how to attach it to the ring in the bull's nose. So he felt safe, even though Dunder was so big and fierce.

The summer was really over. The hay was in the barn and the harvest gathered. But it had turned very warm again. Yonie's shirt was damp from the heat, and his yellow hair clung to his forehead. He wished he could stop work and go wading in the creek.

The Little Conestoga ran through the meadow, and Yonie knew how cool it would be in the shade of the willow tree on its bank. He dropped the bucket he was carrying and started toward the creek. Then he remembered his promise to Pop—and Pop's promise to him. He picked up the bucket and went to pump more water for the rest of the animals and the chickens.

"Ach, vell," he told himself, "I can douse good, once, when I get the chores done."

He grunted as he lifted the heavy pail out of the trough. The water spilled a little onto his bare feet. It felt good and made clean patterns where it washed off the dust. He carried the bucket as full as he could. The chicken pans had to be filled, the calves needed a drink, the pigs had to be fed, and there was still the water to carry in for Granny.

When Yonie had filled the pans in the chicken yard, he made sure to lock the chicken house door. He knew the eggs had been gathered, so he didn't bother to look inside again.

He picked up the buckets in a hurry to water the calves

and then stopped. Was that an airplane he heard? He couldn't see it but now he remembered that Granny wanted the round-wood for the fire.

"Rount-wood gives a hot fire," she had said, "and supper makes soon."

So Yonie went to the woodpile to get it. He could see Nancy under the big tree happily playing with her doll.

He started to gather the wood, and again came the deep purr of an airplane. This time he was sure. It might even be a new kind. He dropped the wood and ran to the corner of the house where he could see better.

As he craned his neck to follow the flight of the plane, he heard Nancy call, "Wonderno-ose Yonie! Wonderno-ose Yonie!" she teased.

He made a face in Nancy's direction, but turned back to

the woodpile. When he carried the wood into the kitchen, Granny wasn't there. Something was bubbling on the stove. It smelled so good! He *must* see what was inside! Could it be apple dumplings? He lifted the lid. Ouch! The steam burned his nose, as usual.

He wondered where Granny could have gone, leaving the supper to cook by itself. But there was more work to do, so he went out to pump water for the calves. The water made him think again of the cool Conestoga. How he wished he were in it!

It wouldn't take long for a splash, he thought, and it

would feel so good! Suddenly he dropped the pump handle and started for the creek. He had his shirt and trousers off almost before he got there, and then—in he went.

The coolness and the quiet murmur of the creek made Yonie stay longer than he meant to. Then in the stillness he heard the bleating of the calves, and suddenly remembered that they were thirsty. He pulled on his clothes as best he could without drying and hurried back to the pump.

When he opened the barnyard gate, the calves came running to get at the water. The little black-and-white one nipped at Yonie's trousers, butted him with his knobbly head, and licked at his hands to see if he had any sugar.

Yonie thought, "That little runt now, if he was mine, I'd call him Wondernose like Pop calls me, the way he's nosing into my hand for sugar! I wish he *was* mine! It would be more fun to water them if one could be mine. If

Pop would give me even a little pig the next time there are any, I'd take care of it till it grew big."

But more than he wanted the calf, more than the little pig, Yonie wanted what Pop had promised. He closed the gate and hurried to get the sour milk for the pigs. He could hear them squealing around beyond the corner of the barn.

When they saw Yonie coming with their supper, they squealed more loudly than ever. There were vegetable parings, bits of bread, and celery tops floating in it. But the pigs thought it was delicious. The great big old sow put both feet in the trough so as to be sure and get her share.

When Yonie went to the kitchen with the water for Granny, she still wasn't there. He thought, once, that he heard her call. But when he listened again he heard nothing.

The food in the kettle had boiled over and didn't smell so good as it had. He called up the stairs, "Granny! Oh, Granny! Somesing smells like burning!" But there was no answer.

He called again, then listened. But there was still no answer. Then he went upstairs and looked in all of the rooms. But still he saw no one and heard nothing. He went downstairs and over into Granny's part of the house.

"Granny!" he shouted, but only the ticking of the clock answered him.

As he stood wondering where Granny might be, his eyes lighted on the painted chest. There Granny kept the old book. It was full of stories that Yonie loved to hear. Granny never allowed the children to open the chest themselves.

She always said, "The things in it are over two hundred years old. That's when your great-great-great-grandfather came with his family and many others from the old country. They came so they might worship God in their own way."

Yonie thought, "It wonders me, now, what else is in there besides the book. I could just look once, and Granny would never know."

He went to the chest where it stood under the window and lifted the lid. But before he could even begin to see anything, he seemed to hear Pop's voice saying, "Yonie! Yonie Wondernose!"

He stood for a second, then was sure that he heard a voice.

It sounded like a real voice coming through the open window.

He listened. He could just barely hear it. But it called, "Yonie! Oh, Yonie!"

He dropped the lid with a bang! Out he flew, through to the kitchen, to the porch, down the yard, through the arbor, and to the chicken house.

Now he could hear the voice plainly, and it was coming from inside the chicken house. "Yonie! Ach, Yonie! Let me out of here!"

He turned the lock and opened the door and out fell Granny! She had been

shut up in the heat of the chicken house ever since Yonie filled the water pans! Yonie helped her to a seat in the arbor and ran to get a drink of water.

When she could speak, she said, "Ach, Yonie! Why didn't you be *this* time a *Wondernose?* Always look *first* inside, *then* lock the door." But Yonie looked so sorry that Granny had to laugh.

"Never mind," she said. "You locked the door like your Pop said. You didn't know Granny was in there. Next time—look inside first." She sniffed the air. "Somesing smells like burning," she said. "Supper, I guess. Ach, vell, ve have spreadin's anyways on our bread, and shoofly pie. Call Nancy."

They went in to supper.

Nancy helped Granny put the "spreadin's" on the table. There was apple butter, currant jelly, stewed apples, and piccalilli. Then there was the pie. It was a shoofly pie made with soft molasses cake baked in a piecrust. Yonie was very fond of it. While they were eating, Granny told how it felt to be shut up in the chicken house.

"Hot as seven in a bed it was in there! I count the

chickens over and over. They stare at me, and cluck like I don't belong in there. And I stare back. I try to get out by the place where the chickens go in, but for a long time now I'm too big for that!"

Yonie and Nancy laughed to think of Granny down on her hands and knees trying to get through that little opening. Yonie thought how it would be to sleep seven in a bed!

"Whew!" he said.

Yonie wished he could douse again in the creek, it was so warm in the kitchen. Granny looked warm, too, and fanned herself with her apron. Even Nancy pushed little wisps of hair up onto her braids.

"It makes like a storm, ain't, Granny?" said Yonie.

"Ya," agreed Granny. "The heat iss something wonderful. It makes a storm, maybe. Make everything fast by the barn."

Nancy ran out to get her doll. And Yonie went to make sure he had done all that Pop told him to do. Yes, he had fed and watered the barn creatures. They were all quiet for the night. When he came in, it was time for him to go to bed.

There was another grumble of thunder, but Yonie didn't hear it. He was asleep.

EDITOR'S NOTE
The promise to which Yonie refers in this excerpt from YONIE WONDERNOSE *is fulfilled at the end of the book. Yonie earns, in a very brave way, too, the right to drive his father's team of horses.*

LAURA INGALLS WILDER

The Sugar Snow

FOR DAYS the sun shone and the weather was warm. There was no frost on the windows in the mornings. All day the icicles fell one by one from the eaves, with soft smashing and crackling sounds. The trees shook their wet, black branches, and chunks of snow fell down.

When Mary and Laura pressed their noses against the cold windowpane they could see the drip of water from the eaves. The snow did not glitter; it looked soft and tired. Under the trees it was pitted where the chunks of snow had fallen, and the banks beside the path were shrinking and settling.

Then one day Laura saw a patch of bare ground in the yard. All day it grew bigger, and before night the whole yard was bare mud. Only the icy path was left, and the snowbanks along the path and the fence and beside the woodpile.

"May I go out to play?" she asked.

"You may tomorrow," Ma promised.

That night Laura woke up, shivering. The bedcovers felt thin, and her nose was icy cold. Ma was tucking another quilt over her.

"Snuggle close to Mary," Ma said, "and you'll get warm."

In the morning the house was warm from the stove, but when Laura looked out of the window she saw that the ground was covered with soft, thick snow. All along the branches of the trees the snow was piled like feathers, and it lay in mounds along the top of the rail fence, and stood up in great, white balls on top of the gateposts.

Pa came in, shaking the soft snow from his shoulders and stamping it from his boots.

"It's a sugar snow," he said.

Laura put her tongue to a bit of the white snow that lay in a fold of his sleeve. It was nothing but wet on her tongue, like any snow. She was glad that nobody had seen her taste it.

"Why is it a sugar snow, Pa?" she asked, but he said he didn't have time to explain now. He must hurry away; he was going to Grandpa's.

Grandpa lived far away in the Big Woods, where the trees were close together and larger.

Laura stood at the window and watched Pa, big and swift and strong, walking away over the snow. His gun was on his shoulder; his hatchet and powder horn hung at his side, and his tall boots made great tracks in the soft snow. Laura watched him till he was out of sight in the woods.

It was late before he came home. Ma had lighted the lamp when he came in. Under one arm he carried a large package, and in the other hand was a big, covered, wooden bucket.

"Here, Caroline," he said, handing the package and the bucket to Ma. Then he put the gun on its hooks over the door.

"If I'd met a bear," he said, "I couldn't have shot him without dropping my load." He laughed. "And if I dropped that bucket and bundle, I wouldn't have had to shoot him. I could have watched him eat what's in them and lick his chops."

Ma unwrapped the package and there were two hard, brown cakes, each as large as a milk pan. She uncovered the bucket, and it was full of dark brown sirup.

"Here, Laura and Mary," Pa said, and he gave them each a little round package out of his pocket.

They took off the paper wrappings, and each had a

Eleanor B.

little, hard, brown cake, with beautifully crinkled edges.

"Bite it," said Pa, and his blue eyes twinkled.

Each bit off one little crinkle, and it was sweet. It crumbled in their mouths. It was better than their Christmas candy.

"Maple sugar," said Pa.

Supper was ready, and Laura and Mary laid the little maple sugar cakes beside their plates, while they ate the maple sirup on their bread.

After supper, Pa took them on his knees before the fire, and told them all about his day at Grandpa's, and all about the sugar snow.

"All winter," Pa said, "Grandpa has been making wooden buckets and little troughs. He made them of cedar, and white ash, for those woods won't give a bad taste to the maple sirup.

"To make the troughs, he split out sticks as long as my hand and as big as my two fingers. Near one end, Grandpa cut the stick half through, and split one half off. This left a flat stick, with a square piece at one end. With a bit he bored a hole lengthwise through the square part. With his knife he whittled the wood till it was only a thin shell around the hole. The flat part of the stick

151

E.B.

he hollowed out with his knife till it was a little trough.

"He made dozens of them, and he made ten new wooden buckets. He had them all ready when the first warm weather came and the sap began to move in the trees.

"Then he went into the maple woods and with the bit he bored a hole in each maple tree, and he hammered the round end of the little trough into the hole, and he set a cedar bucket on the ground under the flat end.

"The sap, you know, is the blood of a tree. It comes up from the roots in the spring, and it goes to the very tip of each branch and twig, to make the green leaves grow.

"Well, when the maple sap came to the hole in the tree, it ran out of the tree, down the trough, and into the bucket."

"Oh, didn't it hurt the poor tree?" Laura asked.

"No more than it hurts you when you prick you finger and it bleeds," said Pa.

"Every day Grandpa goes out into the snowy woods and gathers the sap. With a barrel on a sled, he drives from tree to tree and empties the sap from the buckets into the barrel. Then he hauls it to a big iron kettle that hangs by a chain from a cross timber between two trees.

"He empties the sap into the iron kettle. There is a big bonfire under the kettle and the sap boils, and Grandpa watches it carefully. The fire must be hot enough to keep the sap boiling, but not hot enough to make it boil over.

"Every few minutes the sap must be skimmed. Grandpa skims it with a big, long-handled, wooden ladle that he made of basswood. When the sap gets too hot, Grandpa lifts ladlefuls of it high in the air and pours it back slowly. This cools the sap a little and keeps it from boiling too fast.

"When the sap has boiled down just enough, he fills

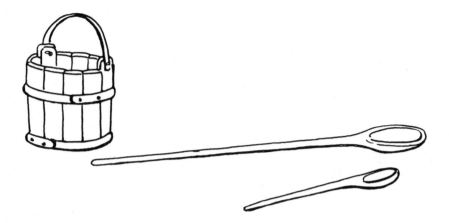

the buckets with the sirup. After that, he boils the sap until it grains when he cools it in a saucer.

"The instant the sap is graining, Grandpa jumps to the fire and rakes it all out from beneath the kettle. Then, as fast as he can he ladles the thick sirup into the milk pans that are standing ready. In the pans the sirup turns to cakes of hard, brown, maple sugar."

"So that's why it's a sugar snow, because Grandpa is making sugar?" asked Laura.

"No," Pa said. "It's called a sugar snow because a snow this time of year means that men can make more sugar. You see, this little cold spell and the snow will hold back the leafing of the trees, and that makes a longer run of sap.

"When there's a long run of sap, it means that Grandpa can make enough maple sugar to last all the year, for common every day. When he takes his furs to town, he will not need to trade for much store sugar. He will get only a little store sugar, to have on the table when company comes."

"Grandpa must be glad there's a sugar snow," Laura said.

"Yes," Pa said, "he's very glad. He's going to sugar off again next Monday, and he says we must all come."

Pa's blue eyes twinkled; he had been saving the best for the last, and he said to Ma:

"Hey, Caroline! There'll be a dance!"

Ma smiled. She looked very happy, and she laid down her mending for a minute "Oh, Charles!" she said.

Then she went on with her mending, but she kept on smiling. She said, "I'll wear my delaine."

Ma's delaine dress was beautiful. It was a dark green, with a pattern over it that looked like ripe strawberries. A dressmaker had made it, in the East, in the place where Ma came from when she married Pa and moved out west

to the Big Woods in Wisconsin. Ma had been fashionable, before she married Pa, and a dressmaker had made her clothes.

The delaine was kept wrapped in paper and laid away. Laura and Mary had never seen Ma wear it, but she had shown it to them once. She had let them touch the beautiful dark red buttons that buttoned the basque up the front, and she had shown them how neatly the whalebones were put in the seams, inside, with hundreds of crisscross stitches.

It showed how important a dance was, if Ma was going to wear the beautiful delaine dress. Laura and Mary were excited. They bounced up and down on Pa's knees, and asked questions about the dance until at last he said:

"Now, you girls run along to bed! You'll know all about the dance, when you see it. I have to put a new string on my fiddle."

156

There were sticky fingers and sweet mouths to be washed. Then there were prayers to be said. By the time Laura and Mary were snug in their trundle bed, Pa and the fiddle were both singing, while he kept time with his foot on the floor:

I'm Captain Jinks of the Horse Marines,
I feed my horse on corn and beans,
And I often go beyond my means,
For I'm Captain Jinks of the Horse Marines,
I'm captain in the army!

Eleanor B.

BETTY BOYLES

Andy's Christmas Zebra

ANDY BOUNCED into the bright, warm kitchen and slammed the back door. The swirling cold wind groaned because it had been shut out from the cozy room. Andy took off his fuzzy, blue cap and rubbed his numb ears. Then he stomped his boots up and down and whacked his mittened hands together.

"Brrr," he shivered. He grinned at his mother who was busy cooking something on the big black stove. "Can I write my letter to Santa Claus right after supper?" he asked.

His mother wadded the hem of her green apron around the frying-pan handle and lifted it off the stove. Andy sniffed at the sizzling fried chicken she carried over to put in the big platter on the table in the center of the room.

"We'll see, Andy. 'Spect so. The men are coming in soon?"

"Yes," said Andy. "I watched 'em brand the new calf, Mother. Daddy said it didn't hurt when they put the hot

iron on the calf. But I'll bet it hurts even the old steers."

His mother poured milk into the glasses on the table. She smiled over at Andy as he took off his red plaid coat.

"It doesn't hurt them long, Andy. It's like pricking yourself with a pin—it hurts just for a minute. We couldn't tell which cows were ours if they didn't get branded. Now run and wash your hands before the men folk come."

A few minutes later Andy was helping his mother put the biscuits on a plate when the men tramped in, clapping their hands and swinging their arms to get warm. Daddy, and Bill, and Oliver, and Mack—all of them huddled around the oven like a bunch of freezing chickens.

At the dinner table Andy tried to keep count of the pieces of chicken Bill ate. He counted out loud every time the short, owl-faced ranch hand asked for more. The other men chuckled when Andy called out "eleven."

160

Andy himself ate only a drumstick. He gulped down his
milk and chewed the turnips and gravy and biscuits as
fast as he could move his teeth. He squirmed in his chair
and watched his father. Finally, when everyone had finished, Andy scooted to the head of the table.

"Daddy," he sputtered, "can I write it tonight? Right
now?"

"Write what?" the tall, thin man with the dark eyes
smiled at the hopeful, tow-headed youngster.

"Why, the letter to Santa Claus. Mother said I could
tonight, right after supper."

"Well," said Daddy, and he looked at Mother, "if you
think it's time, and if you can locate some paper and a
pencil, I guess maybe—"

Andy shrieked and clapped his hands. He rushed to the
chair by the door where he'd thrown his coat when he

came in. He pulled a stubby, yellow pencil and a folded piece of paper out of a pocket. "I've carried it around—just in case."

Mack scratched the fringe of hair around his bald head. "I just don't know about this," he said. "I always heard boys had to be good 'fore they asked Santa Claus to bring 'em something. How about that, Oliver?"

"You're right." Oliver tilted his round ruddy face at Andy. "You done anything you can tell Santa about—anything good, I mean?"

Andy glanced at his mother.

"He's helped me carry in the wood when you all forgot to bring it in," she beamed. "And he's fetched the mail and done lots of other chores."

Andy swallowed and looked at his father. "I've helped

you feed the stock, haven't I, Daddy? And last spring I spaded round the garden."

"Well," Daddy smiled, glancing round the table, "do you men of the bunkhouse agree that he's ready to write it?" Bill and Oliver and Mack nodded.

So Andy picked up the pencil and began to write.

Mother peered over his shoulder as he slowly spelled out the words.

"You've listed all the good things you've done. Now what are you going to ask him to bring you?"

Andy's freckles seemed to light up when he grinned. "It's something I've thought about since summer. Nobody else has one, but I know Santa'll bring it if I ask him."

"Well," Mack laughed, "what in the world is it?"

Andy smiled at all their anxious faces. "I want Santa to bring me—a zebra!"

"A zebra," shouted Bill, looking at Oliver.

"A zebra," shouted Oliver, looking at Mack.

"A zebra," shouted Mack, looking at Andy.

"Yes. A black-striped zebra, like the one at the circus last summer. I want one for Christmas."

"But Andy," Daddy said slowly and carefully, "zebras come from Africa and aren't tame. Santa Claus couldn't get it in his sack. Surely you want something else."

"No." Andy's eyes flickered. "I knew when I saw that zebra that's what I wanted. The keeper said they ran faster'n the wind—faster'n a coyote even."

"Andy." Mother patted his thin shoulders. "Santa can't bring you a wild animal. It wouldn't have room to get in the sleigh."

Andy smiled up at her. "I've got it all thought out. He'll hitch it up with the reindeer. Why it'd outrun any of them. Please, Daddy, spell zebra."

Daddy shrugged his shoulders and spelled the word out slowly. "Z-E-B-R-A. There you are, son. Now I'll get you an envelope."

"Just a minute, Daddy." Andy added, "Thanks," and signed his name.

164

165

Andy clutched the letter to his wool shirt. "How long do you think it'll take, Mother, to get to the North Pole?"

"I—I couldn't say, son. About four or five days, I guess. Andy, you won't be disappointed, will you, if Santa can't bring you a zebra?"

Andy smiled down at the letter. "But he will, Mother. That's all I asked for and I've been good. So he won't mind bringing it to me."

Every night then, after Mother tucked him under the bright, warm quilts, Andy lay awake and thought about the black-and-white striped animal that would be prancing around the corral Christmas morning. How proud he would be to ride like a blizzard across the schoolyard! And all the other children would beg to ride Andy's zebra!

Late one afternoon, a week before Christmas Eve, Andy and Oliver and

Mack pulled up at the back door. In the back of the wagon was a big, crisp green fir tree.

"Mother," Andy shouted as he hopped down from the wagon, "come see our Christmas tree."

The kitchen was dark as he darted inside. Near the door on the little, pine table, he saw a man's wide, black hat and a pair of black gloves. Andy peeked in the parlor, but no one was there. He called for his mother again.

Suddenly quick footsteps whisked down the stairs, and Andy looked up at his father's dark unsmiling eyes.

"We got the tree," Andy shouted. "Come see it. It's bigger'n any we've had. Who's here, Daddy?"

His father led him into the parlor where the fire glowed in the wide brick fireplace.

"Andy," said Daddy, "your mother has had an accident. Doc Lewis is upstairs with her. She's going to be all right, son, but let's not bother her now."

Andy stared at his father. His throat itched, and his blue eyes blinked up and down.

Then Daddy told him how Mother had lifted a pan of boiling water off the stove and how the handle had slipped. Her arms and hands had been scalded when she tried to catch the pan.

"She wouldn't want you to cry," Daddy said. "It would spoil her Christmas if you weren't happy. It won't take long to heal."

Andy didn't cry, not then nor later, when he saw his mother's bandaged arms. He even laughed that night, watching Bill and Daddy cook while Mack and Oliver set the table. But later in bed Andy lay awake a long time, trying to keep the picture of steaming water spilling on Mother out of his mind.

Next morning Andy stumbled down to breakfast. "I want to write another letter to Santa Claus," he said.

"Another one, son?" said Daddy.

"Might not get to the North Pole in time," added Mack.

Oliver smiled. "Isn't a zebra enough to ask for?"

"I've got to write another one." Andy looked with wide eyes at the men. "Please, Daddy."

So Daddy helped with the hard words and this is what Andy wrote:

> Dear Santa Claus,
>
> I wanted a zebra so I could ride fast. Mother burned her arms with boiling water off the stove. Could you bring her a hot-water heater instead of taking time to go by Africa for the zebra? Please Santa. Thank you.
>
> Andrew Palmer

The four big men watched silently while Andy folded the letter. Then Daddy pushed back his chair. "That's a good idea, Andy. Santa will do what he can, I'm sure."

"I'll go mail it for you right now," Bill mumbled.

Early Christmas morning Andy lay in bed under the thick quilts. "It's Christmas morning," he thought, "and I won't have a present from Santa Claus. No prancing, black-and-white zebra dashing round the corral."

Andy sniffled into his pillow, then popped up in bed. Rushing footsteps on the stairs pounded toward his door and in burst Mother, and Mack, and Oliver.

"Merry Christmas, Andy," they shouted. Mother put her bandaged arms around Andy and kissed him. Mack pulled up the window shade so the sun could push inside the little room.

"It's a beautiful Christmas day," Mother said. "Just look out the window at the wonderful Christmas morning!"

Andy slipped into his furry, green slippers and ran to look out the window. He blinked his eyes. There, down by the corral gate, stood Bill. And inside the corral was a live, pudgy, black-and-white striped zebra!

"Mother," Andy squealed. "It's there—the zebra's down there." He shrieked and darted around the room, looking for his clothes.

He struggled into his boots, finally, then looked up at the three pairs of sparkling eyes. "He didn't get my last letter! Mother—you didn't get the heater! Oh—oh—" moaned Andy.

Mother smiled down at the frowning, freckled face. "Santa brought both, son. There was a letter on the tree addressed to me. It's from Santa, and he said a man from Plainfield will come to put the heater in next week."

Andy squealed and streaked down the stairs. He had climbed up on the corral gate beside Bill before Mother and Mack and Oliver could catch up.

Andy stared at the striped animal that was munching hay. A card tied with a blue ribbon was hanging around the zebra's neck. Andy's smile disappeared. The stripes were jagged, not smooth like the circus zebra's. And the ears were big and pointed, not like real zebra's ears.

Andy looked around. He—doesn't look—like a zebra," he mumbled.

"Well, let's see what the card says," Mother said. Oliver hopped inside the corral and untied the ribbon. The zebra looked up with big black eyes but kept on munching the hay.

Mother took the card and read aloud:

> Dear Andrew:
>
> I didn't have time to hunt for a real zebra in Africa. But because you're such a good boy, my workers painted this donkey—so you wouldn't be too disappointed. He does look like a zebra, doesn't he? But, Andy, he can't run fast, so I've brought you a better present. Merry Christmas, and thanks for your letters.
>
> Santa Claus

Andy looked at the donkey again. Then he began to smile, then he giggled, then he laughed. "Ha-ha-ha, a painted donkey!"

Suddenly he heard a clatter of steps running behind him. There from the barn came Daddy. He was leading a frisky, brown pinto pony with a shiny, new saddle. Andy stared, then rushed across the barnyard to meet his father.

170

"Is that it—is that the other present? A pinto!"

"Guess so," Daddy said.

Bill smiled. "I took a quick ride on him, and he's faster than a coyote. Faster than a wild zebra, even, I'll bet."

Andy took the reins from his father and stroked the smooth, broad cheeks of the soft-eyed pony. "Can I get up on him and ride just a little while?"

Daddy helped Andy into the saddle and Andy grinned down into his father's eyes.

"Merry Christmas," he shouted and rode away.

ELIZABETH W. BAKER

Sonny-Boy Sim

ONCE A LONG TIME AGO there was a little log house way off in the piney woods. Right through the middle of the house was the dog-trot. The dog-trot was a wide breezeway, like a hall open at each end, with steps at each end to go in and out.

On one side of the breezeway was a long room with a big fireplace in it, and on the other side were three little bedrooms, each with a bed and a chair.

And three people lived in the little log house in the piney woods.

The first person that lived in the little log house in the piney woods was Grandma. She cooked three meals a day at the big fireplace in the long room. She could make the best corn pone you ever ate. She could roast potatoes in the ashes, and barbecue a turkey on a spit in the fireplace until it would melt in your mouth.

172

Grandma kept the wide planks in the floor scrubbed with water and wood ashes till they were white, almost, as the lacy bedspreads that she knit.

But in the evenings she liked to pull her rocking chair out into the dog-trot and sit there and rock and rest, and knit on a new bedspread. There she would rock and knit, rock and knit, till the moon came up behind the piney woods.

The second person that lived in the little log house in the piney woods was Grandpappy. All day long Grandpappy plowed the corn or hoed the cotton in the fields. In the fall he cut firewood for the big fireplace, and made sweet cider at the cider mill out back of the house.

But in the evenings he liked to pull his highbacked chair out into the dog-trot, and tilt it back against the wall, and rest while he played the fiddle. He was the champion fiddler of all that part of the country. He would cross his knees and play that fiddle, and play that fiddle, till the moon went down behind the piney woods.

The third and last person that lived in the little log house in the piney woods was Sonny-Boy Sim. Sonny-Boy Sim roamed the woods all day with his hound-dog, Homer, chasing a bear or a deer, or sometimes maybe just a black-faced raccoon.

But in the evenings he liked to go out into the dog-trot and dance to the tune of Grandpappy's fiddle. He could bend and turn and leap and clap his hands and lift his feet quicker and lighter than anybody else in all that part of the country. And he would dance to the tune of Grandpappy's fiddle till the moon was sailing through the thin white clouds far above the trees in the dark piney woods.

One day when Sonny-Boy Sim and Homer the hound-

173

dog were out roaming through the piney woods, they came across the biggest black-faced raccoon they had ever seen.

And Homer the hound-dog opened his mouth and let out a note like a deep-toned bell. And Sonny-Boy Sim and Homer the hound-dog lit out after that raccoon and chased him clear down to the bayou. And that raccoon plunged into the water with Homer the hound-dog right after him, close behind.

But just when Homer the hound-dog thought he had that raccoon, here came a pine stump just showing above the water, and that raccoon climbed out of the water onto the pine stump.

And when Homer the hound-dog got right up close to the stump all ready to catch that raccoon, that black-faced raccoon put out his little black hand and pushed that hound-dog's head right down under the water.

When Homer the hound-dog came up again, he turned around and swam back to where he had started from. And when he had climbed onto the bank and shaken off the water and looked back, that black-faced raccoon was sitting on the stump, laughing fit to kill.

Then Sonny-Boy Sim remembered that it was just about dinnertime anyway, so he and Homer the hound-dog ran home to get some of Grandma's good corn pone.

One day Sonny-Boy Sim put on a new straw hat that Grandpappy had bought for him at the store, and he and Homer the hound-dog went off into the piney woods. And the first thing you know they ran across a little black bear cub.

But as soon as it saw them coming, it climbed right up into a pine tree and sat in the crotch of a limb and looked down at them.

174

Now, Sonny-Boy wanted that bear cub for a pet. So he said to himself, "I'll climb that tree and catch that bear cub by the tail, and drop it down to Homer the hound-dog, and we'll take it home and make a pet of it."

So he started climbing up that pine tree.

And when Sonny-Boy Sim got nearly up to where that bear cub was sitting in the crotch of a limb, he reached out his hand to take it by the tail.

But all of a sudden that bear cub opened its mouth and showed all its sharp teeth, and stretched out its long claws and snatched that new straw hat right off Sonny-Boy Sim's head. And Sonny-Boy Sim shinned down that tree a good deal faster than he had climbed up. And when he looked back, that bear cub had Sonny-Boy Sim's new straw hat on its head, and it was laughing fit to kill.

About that time Sonny-Boy Sim thought of that good

sweet apple cider that Grandpappy made, and he and Homer the hound-dog ran home to get some.

Another time when Sonny-Boy Sim and Homer the hound-dog were roaming through the piney woods, they came across a beautiful deer with wide-branching horns. And Homer the hound-dog opened his mouth and let out a note like a deep-toned bell. And he and Sonny-Boy Sim lit out after that deer and chased him till they had him cornered against a high bank of rocks along a creek.

Sonny-Boy Sim thought, "I'll catch the deer and take its horns and make Grandpappy a hatrack out of 'em."

So while Homer the hound-dog barked at the deer's heels, Sonny-Boy Sim reached out to catch that deer by the horns.

But all of a sudden, that deer lowered its head, and with its beautiful wide-branching horns caught Sonny-Boy

176

Sim by his suspenders and threw him right up onto a limb of a big tree.

And then it caught Homer the hound-dog and threw him on top of the bank of rock where a thick grapevine made a soft bed of green. Then the deer stood there for a minute looking at them, laughing fit to kill.

And as it disappeared into the piney woods, Sonny-Boy Sim got to thinking of that good barbecue that Grandma was cooking, and he and Homer the hound-dog climbed down and ran home to get some.

Not long after that, the raccoon and the deer and the bear cub met 'way out in the piney woods.

The deer said, "I'm tired of being chased by Sonny-Boy Sim and his hound-dog Homer."

"So'm I!" said the black-faced raccoon.

"Me, too!" said the bear cub.

"Then," said the deer, "I'll tell you what let's do. Let's get all our sisters and brothers and aunts and uncles and cousins, and go up to that little log house tonight, and show 'em how it feels to be chased about. Let's be there just as the moon is coming up through the piney woods."

That night Grandma pulled her rocking chair out into the dog-trot and got out her knitting. And Grandpappy brought out his high-backed chair and tilted it back against the wall, and began to fiddle. And Sonny-Boy Sim came out and began dancing.

And just as the moon came up behind the piney woods, Homer the hound-dog lifted his head and let out a note like a deep-toned bell. Sonny-Boy Sim ran to the end of the dog-trot to see who was coming.

Then they heard him call, "Grandma! Grandpappy! Come quick!"

So Grandma and Grandpappy ran to the end of the dog-trot where Sonny-Boy Sim was standing.

And there they saw a black-faced raccoon, and a deer with beautiful wide-branching horns, and a black bear cub, all standing out in the yard. And all around them were more raccoons and deer and bears—brothers and sisters and aunts and uncles and cousins.

And you can just better believe that Grandma and Grandpappy and Sonny-Boy Sim were scared!

And when they ran to the other end of the dog-trot and saw more deer and raccoons and bears lined up, they were scared worse than ever.

And Grandpappy said, "Well, they've got us all hemmed in. If they've come here to eat us up, we might as well have one more good time while we can."

So Grandpappy picked up his fiddle and struck up a

lively tune, and Grandma ran back and rolled out a barrel of that good sweet cider.

And Sonny-Boy Sim began to dance, and Homer the hound-dog got up and danced all around Sonny-Boy Sim.

And all those deer and bears and black-faced raccoons came crowding closer and closer, listening to the music and watching Sonny-Boy Sim and Homer the hound-dog dance.

The music got faster and faster, and Sonny-Boy Sim and Homer the hound-dog flung their feet higher and higher.

And presently, all those deer and bears and black-faced raccoons began to sway from side to side in the moonlight, and the first thing you know, they were all dancing together to the tune of Grandpappy's fiddle.

Then Grandma filled a big tub with that good sweet cider, and set it out where they could all drink as much as they liked. And they all danced to the tune of Grandpappy's fiddle till the moon went down behind the piney woods.

And a soft white mist came up from the bayou, and it wrapped itself about all those deer and bears and black-faced raccoons, until, the first thing you know, they all went back into the dark piney woods, laughing fit to kill.

JACK CONROY

The Boomer's Fast Sooner Hound

A BOOMER FIREMAN was an important man on the railroads as far back as the days when they used wood in the firebox to heat up the boilers. His job was a little easier when they changed to coal, but it still took a man with a strong back and wiry arms to shovel all day long with the engine swaying and jerking along the rails.

They called these firemen boomers because they liked to be where business was booming and pay was good. So one year you might find a boomer working on a railroad up in Maine where the boxcars are loaded with potatoes and the next year he'd show up way out in Kansas firing an engine pulling cars filled with yellow wheat.

The boomer firemen were always restless and thinking about a better job on a railroad beyond the high mountains or one that ran alongside the distant sea. They didn't like to stay in one place too long. They didn't need furniture and they didn't need many clothes, and goodness knows they didn't need a family or a dog.

So it looked strange when a boomer fireman walked into a roadmaster's office one fine Spring morning with a long-eared Sooner hound trailing behind him. Why was the dog called a Sooner, did you ask? Well, sir, I'll tell you. It was because that hound would sooner run than eat and he'd sooner eat than fight or do something useful like catching a fat rabbit. Not that a rabbit would have a chance if the Sooner really wanted to nab him, but that hound dog didn't like to do anything but run. And he was the fastest thing on four legs.

"I might be able to use you," said the Roadmaster when the Boomer asked for a job. "Where'll you keep your dog?"

"Oh, he goes along with me," answered the Boomer.

"I raised him from a pup just like I was his mother and father rolled into one. He's never spent a day or even an hour away from me. He'd cry like his poor heart would break if I left him, and he'd make such a racket that nobody could sleep, eat, or hear themselves think for forty miles about."

"Well, I don't see how that would work out," said the Roadmaster, shaking his head. "It's against the rules of this railroad to allow a passenger—man, woman, child or beast—in the cab or in the caboose. In fact, it's Rule Number One in the rule book. I aim to put you on a freight train, so you can't ship him in the express car. Besides, when he found out you weren't anywhere around he'd pester folks to death with his yipping and yowling. You look to me like a man that could keep a boiler popping off steam on an uphill grade, but I don't see how we can work it if the hound won't listen to reason and stay quietly behind while you're away on your runs."

"Why, he's no trouble!" cried the Boomer. "He just runs alongside the train, and when I'm on a freight run he chases around a little in the fields to pass the time away. It's a little bit tiresome for him to have to travel at such a slow gait, but that Sooner, he'd do anything to stay close by me."

> "That may be so, I do not know;
> It sounds so awful queer.
> I don't dispute your word at all,
> But don't tell that yarn in here,"

sang the Roadmaster.

"He'll do it without half trying," said the Boomer calmly. "I'll put up my first paycheck against a five dollar bill that he'll be fresh as a daisy and his tongue will be behind

his teeth when we pull up at the junction. He'll run around
that station a hundred times or so to limber up after having
to go at such a slow pace."

"It's a bet," said the Roadmaster. "This will be just like
taking candy from a baby."

On the first run the Sooner moved in what was a slow
trot for him. He stopped to dig after moles and gophers in
the fields and sometimes spent a minute or two barking
friendly greetings to other dogs near farmhouses. Now and
then he would sidle over and look up at the engine with an
anxious look on his face.

"What's the matter with him?" asked the engineer.

"He's worried about the law that says you must stop the

train wherever you are after you've been on the road ten hours or more," answered the Boomer, setting down his shovel and wiping the sweat off his face. "He's afraid we'll have to stop way out in the middle of nowhere. It's all because he thinks we're not making good enough time. That dog is true blue as they come, and he has the interests of the railroad at heart just because I work for it."

"You don't tell me!" cried the engineer. "This train is going faster than it ever has before. If it goes any faster it'll jump the track."

"It may be fast for the train, but it's slow for my Sooner," declared the Boomer. "He's the fastest thing on four legs. He wouldn't need more than one of them to beat this slow-poke train."

The Roadmaster was so angry at losing the bet that he threw his cap to the ground and jumped up and down on it about fourteen times before he could say a word.

"Put the Boomer on a local passenger train," he ordered,

"and I'm going to double the bet. No flea-bitten hound is going to make a monkey out of me and this railroad."

The Sooner had to speed up to a slow gallop once in a while when he was following the local passenger train, but he had to kill a lot of time, at that, so as not to get too far ahead of the engine.

Then the Roadmaster really lost his temper. People watched the Sooner running lazily alongside the train and began thinking that it must be a mighty slow railroad. Passengers could *walk* from one town to another in less time, they complained. And if you shipped a yearling calf to market it'd be too tough to eat before it reached the stockyards.

Of course, the trains were keeping up their schedules the same as usual, but that's the way it looked to folks who saw a no-good, mangy Sooner hound outrunning all the trains without his tongue hanging out an inch or letting out the least little pant.

The Sooner was giving the railroad a bad name, all right. The Roadmaster would have fired the Boomer and told him to take his hound and go far away to some place else on the other side of the mountains or even beyond the deep blue sea, but he was a proud man and a stubborn one and he hated worse than anything to own up that he had been bested.

"I'll fix that Sooner!" he said, after sulking for a week and four days. "I'll put the Boomer in the cab of the Cannon Ball Limited. It's the fastest thing on wheels. The Sooner hound is the fastest thing on four legs, but if he can even keep within sight of the Cannon Ball I'll be the first to take off my cap to him. That no-good, lop-eared hound will be left so far behind it'll take nine dollars and eighteen cents to send him a post card."

Word got around that the Sooner was going to try to keep up with the Cannon Ball. Farmers left off plowing, hitched up, and drove miles to the railway tracks to see the sight. The schools all dismissed their pupils, and not a factory could keep enough men to make a wheel turn. It was like circus day or the county fair.

The Roadmaster climbed right up in the cab to make sure that the Boomer kept up plenty of steam. A clear track was ordered for a hundred and six miles, twelve feet, and eleven inches. All the switches were spiked down tight until after the Cannon Ball had passed by.

It took three men to see the Cannon Ball on that run: one to say, "There she comes," one to say, "There she is," and another to say, "There she goes."

You couldn't see your hand before your eyes there was

so much steam, cinders, and smoke in the air. The rails sang like a violin for a half hour after the Cannon Ball had passed into the next county.

Every safety valve was popping off steam and the wheels rose three feet in the air above the rails. The Boomer was so sure that the Sooner could keep up that he shoveled away with all his might. He wore the hinges off the fire door, and fifteen pounds of him melted and ran right down into his shoes. His shovel was whetted down to a nub.

The Roadmaster poked his head out of the window, and—whoosh!—off went his cap and his head almost followed. The suction nearly jerked his arms from their sockets as he held onto the window seat for dear life. It was all he could do to see anything, and gravel pinged against his goggles like hailstones. He let out a whoop of joy.

"THE SOONER! THE SOONER!" he yelled. "He's gone! He's gone!"

"I can't understand that," hollered the Boomer. "It just isn't like that Sooner to lay down on me at all. Let *Me* take a peek."

He dropped his shovel and stuck his head out the window. Sure enough, the Sooner was nowhere in sight. The Boomer's troubled gaze swept far and wide.

"Don't see hide nor hair of him, do you?" demanded the Roadmaster. "He's at least sixty-four and maybe seventy-six miles behind."

The Boomer said nothing. He just pulled his head back into the cab and began to shovel coal into the firebox. He worked without much spirit, shaking his head in a puzzled way. There was no need for hard work, anyhow, since the Cannon Ball was pulling into the station at the end of the run.

Before the wheels had stopped rolling, the Roadmaster leaped nimbly to the ground. A big cheer was heard from a group of people nearby. The Roadmaster ran over and elbowed his way among them.

"Here I am," he announced. "Where are all the cameras and the newspaper reporters? I'll climb back in the cab if you think I'd make a better picture there. Besides, we ought to get the Cannon Ball in it."

"Go away and don't bother us," said a man, turning toward the railroad official. "You might as well sell that Cannon Ball for scrap iron. It's slower than the 'Slow Train

through Arkansaw,' and that's about as slow as a locomotive can get and still be moving."

"She's fast enough to leave that mangy, lop-eared Sooner hound at least sixty-four and maybe seventy-six miles behind," boasted the Roadmaster.

"You're crazy with the heat!" jeered the man. "That true blue Sooner has been here a good half hour and time has been hanging heavy on his hands. Take a look!"

Then the Roadmaster saw that the crowd wasn't looking toward him at all but at something inside a circle it had formed around a persimmon tree. The Roadmaster pushed his way through. The Sooner was loping lazily around the tree, barking at an angrily spitting cat which had climbed for safety among the upper branches. The Sooner didn't look the least bit tired, and his tongue was behind his teeth.

"I'm through, good people and little children!" sputtered the Roadmaster. "I'm willing to hoist the white flag and call it quits. Rule Number One is done away with right here and now. Let the Sooner ride in the cab as often and as far as he wants to."

"That's real nice of you, boss," declared the Boomer, shaking the Roadmaster's limp hand. "The Sooner and I both appreciate it. Well, if you'll climb back in the cab and the engineer is ready we'll be on our way back."

The engineer tooted his whistle twice to show he was ready.

"I don't want to ride," replied the Roadmaster sorrow-fully. "I'd rather walk."

The Cannon Ball chugged away from the station with the Boomer waving his shovel about his head and the Sooner yelping proudly beside him. The people cheered until the train was out of sight. Nobody noticed the Road-master as, with downcast head and careful feet, he stepped from tie to tie along the track on the long road home.